SOUL HEIGHTS AND SOU..,

BY

Octavius Winslow

SOUL HEIGHTS AND SOUL DEPTHS

Published by Scriptura Press

New York City, NY

First published circa 1878

Copyright © Scriptura Press, 2015

All rights reserved

ABOUT SCRIPTURA PRESS

Scriptura Press is a Christian company that makes Christian works available and affordable to all. We are a non-denominational publishing group that shares the teachings of the Scripture, whether in the form of sermons or histories of the Church.

Soul Heights and Soul Depths

Soul Depths

"Out of the depths have I cried unto You, 0 Lord." — Psalm 130:1.

It is of little moment to our present exposition that we determine the precise occasion in David's history on which this Psalm was composed. Suffice, that it forms one of the richest and most tuneful of his poetical compositions, and unfolds one of the most spiritual and instructive chapters in his remarkable history. As such, it reflects the lights and shadows, the depths and heights of the Christian life, as more or less vividly portrayed in every believer's history. That there are these opposites of soul-exercise in the experience of all the spiritual seed of David, of all to whom belong his "sure mercies"— not excepting David's Lord— the history of the Church of God fully attests.

The Christian life is tortuous and chequered in its course. The royal path to glory is a divine mosaic paved with stones of diverse lines. Today, it is a depth almost soundless; tomorrow, a height almost scaleless. Now, a shadow drapes the picture, somber and rayless; then, a light illumines the camera, brilliant and gladsome. Here, the "song" is of mercy, sweet and entrancing; there, it is of judgement, sad and mournful. "When men are cast down, then you shall say, There is lifting up." But, a divine Hand, veiled and invisible to all but faith's eye, shapes and directs the whole; and, assured of this, the believing soul is trustful and calm.

"He led them about, He instructed them," was the history of the Church in the wilderness; and each stage was a school, each condition a blessing, each event a lesson learned, and a new beatitude experienced,— learned and experienced as in no other. Variety, rich and endless, is stamped upon all God's works and operations; not less is this seen in the circuitous path by which He is leading His people home to Himself. It is this ever-dissolving, ever shifting scenery of the Christian's life that unfolds new views of God's character, and brings him into a closer acquaintance with his own.

To the consideration, then, of these "depths" and "heights" of the Christian life, let us now devoutly and thoughtfully address ourselves. And may the Eternal Spirit unfold and apply His truth to the edification of the reader, and to the glory of His own name, for Christ Jesus' sake! "Out of the depths have I cried unto you, 0 Lord."

It may be proper to intimate in the commencement of our treatise, that the experience described in this, its opening chapter, must not be interpreted as that of an unregenerate soul. That there are "depths" of temporal adversity and mental distress, deep and dark, in the life of the unregenerate, is manifest; but, they are not the "depths" of God's people. It is recorded of the wicked who prosper in the world, that they have "no changes in their life," and "no bands in their death, and are not as other men." But the saints of God dwell among their own people, and walk in paths untrodden by the ungodly. The experience, then, which we are about to describe is peculiar to the saints.

However profound these 'depths,' they are not the depths of hell, draped with its mist of darkness, and lurid with its quenchless flames. There is in them no curse, nor wrath, nor condemnation. Sink as the gracious soul may, it ever finds the Rock of Ages beneath, upon which faith firmly and securely stands. Whatever may be the depressions of the believer, it is important to keep in mind his real standing before God. From this no chequered spiritual history can move him. There is not an angel in heaven so divinely related, so beauteously attired, or who stands so near and is so dear to God, as the accepted believer in Christ, though earth is still his abode, and a body of sin his dwelling.

A practical lesson grows out of this truth. Let it be your aim to know your present standing as in the sight of God. Upon so vital a question not the shadow of a doubt should rest. "We believe, and are sure." Faith brings assurance, and assurance is faith. The measure of our assured interest in Christ, will be the measure of our faith in Christ. This is the true definition of assurance, the nature of which is a question of much perplexity to sincere Christians. Assurance is not something audible, tangible, or visionary— a revelation to the mind, or a voice in the air. Assurance is believing. Faith is the cause, assurance is the effect. Assurance of personal salvation springs from looking to, and dealing only with Jesus. It comes not from believing that I am saved, but from believing that Christ is my Savior.

The object of my salvation is not my faith, but Christ. Faith is but the instrument by which I receive Christ as a sinner. As the eaglet acquires strength of vision by gazing upon the sun, until at length, when fledged, it expands its wings and soars to the orb of day,— so the eye of faith, by "looking unto Jesus" only, gradually becomes stronger; and in proportion to its clear and still clearer view of Christ, brings increased, sweet, and holy assurance to the soul.

One simple, believing sight of Christ will produce more light and peace and joy than a lifetime of looking within ourselves for evidences and signs of grace. All the sinner's merit, all his worthiness, beauty, and salvation, is centered in Christ, is from Christ, and Christ alone. And, by simply believing the great truth of the gospel, that Christ died for sinners— receiving Christ, not purchasing Him,— as God's "unspeakable gift" of free and sovereign grace, will awaken in the soul the assured and grateful acknowledgment, "He loved me, and gave Himself for me." But let us enumerate some of those soul-depths into which many of God's people are frequently plunged, in which grace sustains, and out of which love delivers them. "Out of the depths have I cried unto you, 0 Lord."

We place in the foreground of these "depths," as constituting, perhaps, the most common— soul-distress arising from the existence and power of indwelling sin in the regenerate. There is not a fact in the history of the saints more clearly taught or more constantly verified than this: that, while the Holy Spirit renews the soul, making it a new creature in Christ Jesus, He never entirely uproots and slays the principle and root of sin in the regenerate. The guilt of sin is cleansed by atoning blood, and the tyranny of sin is broken by the power of divine grace, and the condemnation of sin is cancelled by the free justification of Christ; nevertheless, the root, or principle of original sin remains deeply and firmly embedded in the soil, ever and anon springing up and yielding its baneful fruit, demanding unslumbering watchfulness and incessant mortification; and will so remain until death sets the spirit free.

The inhabitants of Canaan were allowed by God still to domicile in the land long after His chosen people had entered and possessed it. They were to contract no covenant with them, either by marriage or commerce; but, laid under tribute, they were to remain subject to a gradual process of extermination, contributing to, rather than taking from, the wealth and power of Israel's tribes. This is an impressive and instructive emblem of the regenerate! The old inhabitants still domicile in the new creature: original sin, individual corruption, and constitutional infirmity— surviving the triumphant advent of the converting grace of God— often challenging the forces of the Most High, and inflicting upon the soul many a deep and grievous wound.

Now, it is the existence of this fact that constitutes a source of so much soul-distress to the regenerate, bringing them into those "depths" familiar to the most gracious. When the Holy Spirit inserts the plough more deeply into the corrupt soil of the heart, turning up the fair surface, and revealing the hidden, deeply- seated, and but little-suspected, evil— the law of corruption for a moment stronger than the law of grace, the law of the flesh obtaining a temporary ascendancy over the law of the Spirit— then rises the dolorous lamentation out of the depths: "0 wretched man that I am! who shall deliver me from the body of this death? 0 Lord, out of the depths of my deep corruption I call unto You! My soul is plunged into great and sore troubles by reason of indwelling sin, whose name is 'legion'— pride, self-righteousness, carnality, covetousness, worldliness— working powerfully and deceitfully in my heart, and bringing my soul into great straits and fathomless depths of sorrow."

Beloved, when first you found the Savior, you imagined that the warfare had ceased, that the victory was won, and that, henceforth, your Christian course would be a continuous triumph over every foe, your path to heaven smooth and cloudless, until lost in perfect day! But your real growth in grace is the measure of your growing acquaintance with yourself. A deeper knowledge of your sinfulness, a more intimate acquaintance with the subterfuges of your own heart, has changed your paean of triumph into well-near a wail of despair; has hurled you as from the pinnacle to the base of the mount; and from the base, into a "depth" yet deeper you never supposed to exist, and out of which— the "slough of despond"— your cry of agony ascends to God.

But, deem not your case a solitary one; nor be surprised, as though some strange thing had happened unto you. Such "depths" have all the saints. All are taught in this school; all are brought into the region of their own heart, where their holiest and most experimental lessons are learned. Let not, then, the existence, sight, and conflict of the indwelling of sin plunge you in despair; rather, accept it as an unmistakable evidence of your possession of the divine nature, of the living water welled in your soul- the existence and warfare of which have but revealed to you the counter existence and antagonism of the latent and deep-seated evil of your heart.

But, not the indwelling of sin only, still more its outbreaking, describes another soul-depth of God's saints. What an evidence have we here of the truth just insisted upon— the indwelling power of sin in the regenerate! Truly, were there no indwelling root of sin, there would be no outgrowing fruit of sin. The mortification of sin in its principle, would be the mortification of sin in its practice. The death of sin in the heart of the Christian would, necessarily, be the death of sin in the life of the Christian. No fact more logical or self-evident. But where is the true believer who, as before a heart-trying God, can claim the entire uprooting of the indwelling principle of evil— who, unless awfully self-deceived, can in truth assert that he has arrived at such a degree of sanctification as to live a day, an hour, a moment, a sinless life?

How contrary would such vain boasting be to the recorded experience of the most matured believer- the most advanced and holy Christian! Listen to the language of David: "Wash me throughly from mine iniquity, and cleanse me from my sin. For I acknowledge my transgressions and my sin is ever before me." Listen to job: "I abhor myself, and repent in dust and ashes." Listen to Peter: "Depart from me; for I am a sinful man, O Lord." Listen to Paul: "Sinners; of whom I am chief." Who, with such examples before him, will profanely claim perfect freedom, not merely from the indwelling existence, but from the outbreaking effects of sin?

But who can fully describe the soul-sorrow; one of the profoundest depths of the regenerate occasioned by the consciousness of sinful departure from God? "And Peter went out, and wept bitterly." The penitence of Peter was a type of all true penitents, whose backslidings the foregoing acknowledgments recall to remembrance. And what a mercy that our Heavenly Father does not leave His wandering child to the hardening tendency and effect of his backslidings; but, sooner or later, His Spirit, by the word, or through some afflictive discipline of love, recalls the wanderer to His feet, with the confession and the prayer- "O Lord, pardon my iniquity; for it is great." "Heal me, O Lord, and I shall be healed." These confessions of sin what gracious soul does not echo? Surely every heart that knows its own plague will make them its own; and thus the Holy Spirit fashions our renewed hearts alike.

There are also "depths" of mental darkness and despondency into which gracious souls fall. Many a shaded and lonely stage of the Christian's pilgrimage lies in the way to heaven. Through many a dark, starless night the spiritual voyager ploughs the ocean to the desired haven where he would be. It is far more the province of faith to work and travel and sail in the dark than in the light, in the night season than the day. And thus, this essential and precious principle of the regenerate soul is put to a more crucial and certain test than when the path of the believer is decked with smiling flowers and radiant with unclouded sunshine. It is, "Faith in the dark, Pursuing its mark Through many sharp trials of love."

In the family of God there are not a few Christians of a morbidly religious tendency of mind, whose Christian career through life is seldom relieved and brightened by a solitary thrill of joy or ray of hope. While the reality of their conversion is undoubted by all but themselves, they seem to have settled down into a spiritual state of despondency and despair in which all evidence is ignored, all comfort refused, and all hope extinguished. In vain you unfold the gospel in all the fullness of its message, the freeness of its overtures, and the preciousness of its promises. They repel you with the reply that its provisions, invitations, and comforts are for others but not for them; that theirs is not the blessedness of those for whom these glad tidings are sent.

Tell them of God's great love in the gift of His Son of Christ saving sinners to the uttermost, rejecting none who come to Him; of the blood that has a sovereign efficacy in its cleansing from all sin; remind them that, when God begins a work of grace in the soul of a poor sinner, He never leaves it incomplete; that, although the sun in the firmament is often obscured by a cloud, yet all the while it shines as intensely brilliant as though not a shadow veiled its light; and that thus it is with the Sun of Righteousness and the child of the light walking in darkness; you but deal with a believer on whose brow the "agony of anxious helplessness" is stamped.

But until a power infinitely mightier than the human is exerted, morbid melancholy will still claim the victim as its own. Religious delusion is the great characteristic of souls in a state of morbid religiousness. But is there no remedy? Has not the gospel its appropriate instructions and helps for a soul thus overshadowed and depressed? Surely there are divine steps out of this "depth," might we but succeed in unveiling them to the desponding eye. Our true process will be to trace it to some of its more fruitful and proximate causes, the discovery and statement of which may suggest more than half its remedy. To this attempt let us address ourselves.

We do not hesitate placing in the foreground of causes producing spiritual despondency, one which, perhaps, is the most common, though the least suspected of all- the physical constitution and state of the afflicted one. In this case the physician who prescribes for the body, rather than he who ministers to the soul, may be the most appropriate and useful adviser. So intimately united are the two constituent parts of our organism- mind and body, there must necessarily be a continuous action and reaction of the one upon the other; and the peculiar condition in which both may be at that moment, must of necessity, exert a powerful and reciprocal influence.

Now, in numberless cases of morbid religious despondency the cause is purely physical. This may, perhaps, shock the piety of some, and not the less supply ground of attack upon religion on the part of others; nevertheless, the psychological fact remains the same. A disturbed and unhealthy condition of any one vital organ of the body, may so powerfully act upon the mind, and that in its turn upon the Soul, as to tinge the mental and moral perceptions, distort the most simple truths, embitter the sweetest consolations, and shade the brightest hopes and prospects of the soul.

Depressed child of God, suffering from this cause, be of good cheer! The Lord, who loves you- loves you not less when all is dark as when all is light- knows your frame, and remembers that you are dust. Your present mental cloud-veil does not, and cannot, extinguish the heavenly light within you, touch your spiritual life, or separate you from the love of God, which is in Christ Jesus your Lord. The divine nature, of which you are, through grace, a partaker, rises as far above the condition of the body as the infinite rises above the finite. The spiritual life of your soul flows from, and is bound up with, the life of God in heaven.

And if there is any gentleness and sympathy in Christ (and who can doubt it?) which clusters with a deeper intensity around a child of His love, it is he who, suffering from physical disease, pain, and languor, is at the same moment battling, as an effect, with morbid religiousness and mental despondency; and these, in their turn, gendering spiritual doubts and distress touching the happiness of the present, and the hope of the future. Little think we with what tenderness and gentleness Jesus deals with the 'sick one whom He loves,' and what consideration and forbearance He exercises towards those who, through bodily infirmity and physical suffering, are plunged into depths of religious melancholia, bordering, it may be, on the very verge of despair and self-destruction! Jesus, who built your frame, remembers that you are dust;' and from no heart in the universe pulsating with love towards you, flows such intelligent compassion, such patience, forbearance, and tender sympathy as from Christ's.

But there are spiritual causes yet more potent- to which this morbid, self-condemning action of the mind may be traced. Let us glance at one or two of them. The substitution, for example, of the work of the Spirit in the soul, for the work of Christ for the soul, supplies a fruitful cause of religious doubt and despondency in many Christians. God, in the exercise of His grace, never intended that the sources of our Christian evidence and spiritual fertility should be within ourselves. It was His purpose to lodge our entire salvation in Christ; at the same time leaving undisturbed our individual responsibility and duty to "give all diligence to make our calling and election sure;" and thus "work out our own salvation with fear and trembling," encouraged by the assurance, that it is "God that works in us to will and to do of His good pleasure."

To look, then, within ourselves for spiritual light, joy, and hope, is just as unwise and vain as to put sound for substance, the sun reflected from the bosom of a lake, for the sun blazing in mid-heaven. It is to Christ obeying and suffering, bleeding and dying for us, that we are to look for our evidences, fruitfulness, and hope, and not to the work of the Holy Spirit wrought in our souls. Essential to our renewal and sanctification as is the work of the Spirit, He did not atone for us. He is not our Savior, nor His work our salvation, necessary and precious as is His office in the economy of Redemption.

Christ alone is our Redeemer, His righteousness our justification, His blood our pardon, His merits our standing before God; and it is looking to Him in faith, to His mediation, merits, and fullness, that we arrive at any degree of spiritual evidence, fruitfulness, and assurance. Turning within yourself for marks and signs of grace, and finding instead nothing but sin, and darkness, and change, how are you to become a firm believer and a joyful Christian? Looking to your experience, your fitful frames and feelings, and not by faith to Christ, the wind is not more capricious, nor the tide more changeful, than will be your peace and comfort, your holiness and hope.

But, try the experiment of looking away from yourself to Jesus. Pass by even the cross, the atonement, the gospel, and the sacrament, and rest not until you find yourself face to face, heart to heart, with a PERSONAL, living, loving SAVIOR, -the gracious words breathing in sweetest cadence from His lips- Oh listen to their music, you sin-disturbed, soul-desponding ones!– "Come unto ME, all you that labor and are heavy-laden, and I will give you REST." "Look unto ME, all the ends of the earth, and be saved: for I am God, and there is none else." "I am the door;" "I am the bread of life." In all these gracious invitations we hear the voice of a Personal- "I AM" -of a Personal Savior.

Cease, then, to deal with dogmas, feelings and experience, however elevated or depressed, and behold the Lamb of God, contemplate His Person, study His work, feast upon His word, revel in His fulness, bathe in the sea of His love, and let Him be all in all to your soul. Thus turning the eye from yourself and dealing only with the Person of Jesus, the cloud will uplift from your mind, "the winter will depart, and the flowers appear, the time of the singing of birds will come, and the voice of the turtle be heard in the land;" and your soul, thus bursting from its icy fetters, its wintry sterility and gloom, into the beauty and fragrance of its new spring-life of joy, will be "Like the sweet south wind, that breathes upon a bank of violets, Stealing and giving odors."

In how many cases this spiritual despondency may be traced to the idea, incessantly haunting the mind, of having committed the unpardonable sin, the sin against the Holy Spirit! But how groundless this fear! Apart from the probability, and we might in a qualified sense add, the impossibility, of the fact, the holy fear and trembling which the apprehension creates, is of itself a sufficient contradiction of such a thing. But, what was the sin against the Holy Spirit which Jesus denounced in terms so appalling? Clearly, it was that of ascribing to the agency of Satan the Divine power by which He wrought His wonderful miracles. "This fellow does not cast out devils but by Beelzebub, the prince of the devils." Then said Jesus, "All sins shall be forgiven to the sons of men ... But he that shall blaspheme against the Holy Spirit has never forgiveness, but is in danger of eternal damnation."

Such clearly was the sin against the Holy Spirit. Can it be yours, my reader? Impossible! You have never been tempted, or if tempted have never yielded to the temptation for a moment- loathing and rejecting it– of ascribing the Divine works of Christ to Satanic power! Oh no! Banish, then, from your mind the appalling thought, this groundless fear; and clasp in the arms of your faith and love afresh the gracious, sin-atoning, sin-forgiving Savior, who has never permitted you to fall into this 'depth of Satan,' and who will, with the temptation, give you grace, that you may be able to bear and victoriously to repel it.

Others of God's saints are often plunged into great depths of soul distress, occasioned by the doctrine of Election. Through the misrepresentations of some teachers, and their own crude notions of the doctrine, they extract bitterness from one of the sweetest and clearest truths of God's word. But, divine and precious as the doctrine of Election is, it is not a truth with which we have immediately to do in the great matter of personal salvation. Election belongs to God alone; it is His eternal and profound secret, with which we have nothing to do but unquestionably to believe. "Secret things belong to God;" and this is one of the most profoundly secret. The truth with which we have to do is our effectual calling; this made sure, the certainty of our election follows; our calling is the effect and consequence of our election. Hence the order in which the Holy Spirit, by the apostle, places these truths: "Be diligent to make your calling and election sure."

The first and lowest link in the chain of your salvation is your calling by the Spirit. Called by sovereign grace to see your sinfulness, to accept Christ; and evidencing the reality of your calling by a pure and holy life, you have made sure of the last and the highest link of the chain, and may calmly leave the fact of your eternal election to everlasting life with God, in whose hands it is alone and safely lodged. With the divine decrees, happily, you have nothing to do. You are not called to believe that you are one of the elect; but you are called to believe in Jesus Christ- that you are a poor, lost sinner, feeling your need of the Savior, looking only to His blood and righteousness as the ground of your pardon, justification, and final glory. Thus called by grace to be a saint of God, election will become to you one of the most encouraging, comforting, and sanctifying doctrines of the Bible.

Cease, then, to trouble your soul as to this divine and hidden truth, and deal directly and only with Christ. Then will your soul, ascending from this 'depth' of doubt and despondency in which too long you have lain, and rising into the region of light, joy and hope, will sing as you soar- "My soul is escaped as a bird out of the snare of the fowler: the snare is broken, and I am escaped." "Whom He did predestinate, them He also called: and whom He called, them He also justified: and whom He justified, them He also glorified."

The word of God speaks of the "depths of Satan" (Rev. 2:24). Some of these "depths" mark the experience of many of the saints. The members of Christ's body must, in a great degree, be conformed to their Head; and no chapter of our Lord's life is more instructive than that of His temptation in the wilderness. "Tempted in all points like as we are," He thus, during those forty days' and forty nights' conflict with the devil, was learning how to succor those who are tempted. There are "depths" in Satan's temptations of various degrees; some deeper and darker than others. Some of the Lord's people are tempted to doubt, and almost to deny, the work of grace in their soul; some are tempted to limit the power and willingness of Christ to save them; others are attacked in the very citadel of their faith, sorely tempted to deny the truth of God's word, the veracity of His character, and a future life beyond the grave. How many saints there are whose temptations lie within the circle of their families; others within the sphere of their calling in life; others in their service for Christ; and not a few within the very church of God itself!

There is no part of the Christian armor so invulnerable which Satan will not attempt to pierce, and no place so retired or engagement so holy where his "depths" are not concealed! Are you thus tempted, child of God? Have you fallen into some of these "depths of Satan"? "Beloved, think it not strange concerning the fiery trial which is to try you, as though some strange thing happened unto you;" for, "there has no temptation taken you but what is common to man: but God is faithful, who will with the temptation also make a way to escape, that you may be able to bear it." The Lord will not leave you to perish in these wiles or to sink in these depths of Satan; but while in them will instruct you in truths, and teach you lessons, learned only in this fiery and trying school and, when spiritually and effectually learned, He will 'pull you out of the net,' and raise you above the 'depths,' more perfectly assimilated than ever to the image of your Lord, once tempted in all points like as you are; and who knows how to succor those who are thus tempted.

We must not omit the depths of affliction and trial into which, more or less profound, all the Lord's people are plunged. The language of David, and of David's Lord, is that of all the spiritual seed of David: "Deep calls unto deep at the noise of your waterspouts: all your waves and your billows are gone over me." Deep and billowy and dark are often the waters through which the saints wade to glory. "The Lord tries the righteous;" and He tries them because they are righteous, and to make them yet more righteous still. It was deep in the fathomless depths that Jonah learned the most precious of all truths: "Salvation is of the Lord." It was in the cave of Adullam- in the lion's den- in the noisome pit in the jail of Philippi- in the isle of Patmos- in the garden of Gethsemane; that David, and Daniel, and Jeremiah, and John, and Jesus, were brought into the richest teaching, holiest lessons, and most blessed experience of their lives.

And shall we, beloved, plead exemption from these depths of trial, tribulation, and sorrow? Ah no! what losers should we be were it so! Who would not follow in the footsteps of the flock? Above all, who would not walk in the footsteps of the Shepherd of the flock, who, though He were a Son, yet learned He obedience by the things which He suffered"? Look up, then, you sinking child of sorrow! Are you enquiring of the Lord, "Why am I thus tried, thus afflicted, thus chastened?" Listen to His answer: "As many as I love, I rebuke and chasten."

Reader, resolve all this discipline of trial and of sorrow through which your God is calling you to pass- the loss that has

lessened your resources, the bereavement that has broken your heart, the trial that has saddened your spirit, the temptation that has assailed your faith- into the everlasting and unchangeable love of your Father in heaven. "For whom the Lord loves He chastens, and scourges every son whom He receives." Therefore, "despise not you the chastening of the Lord, nor faint when you are rebuked of Him."

Out of the depths of affliction and sorrow the Lord will hear your cry, and from them will raise you. The promise will stand good to the end- the promise upon which many a soul, sinking in deep waters, has clung with faith's undying grasp: "When you pass through the waters, I will be with you; and through the rivers, they shall not overflow you: when you walk through the fire, you shall not be burned; neither shall the flame kindle upon you." Welcome, O welcome, the sanctified discipline of trial and sorrow that proves your conversion real, your title to heaven valid, and your hope in Jesus such as will not expire when the cold damps of death are gathering around it; but will become stronger and more luminous as the lamps of earth recede and fade, and those of heaven approach nearer and grow more bright. Lord, if your furnace thus refines and your knife thus prunes- rendering your "gold" more pure and your "branch" more fruitful

"Let me never choose or to live or die,

Bind or bruise, in your hands I lie."

Not anticipating the subject of the next chapter, we would close the present by reminding the believer thus exercised that, as sure as there are in the experience of the saints 'depths' of soul-trouble and conflict, depths of spiritual and mental despondency and despair, 'depths' of trial and sorrow, 'depths' of temptation and need- "a night and a day in the deep" -so there are deliverances; and in God's own time those deliverances will come. "Cast not away therefore your confidence, which has great recompense of reward."

Did the Lord ever leave His child to flounder and sink and perish in his 'depths'? Never! He invariably sends help from above, takes them in His arms, and gently draws them out of their 'many waters,' just as He lifted up Joseph from the deep pit, and Daniel from the lions' den, and Jeremiah from the loathsome dungeon. Cheer up then, you sinking, desponding one! Behold the bright stars that shine and sing above your head- those "exceeding great and precious promises" of God, "which are all yes and Amen in Christ Jesus;" and behold the "rainbow in the clouds" - the symbol and pledge of God's covenant faithfulness to make good those promises, and deliver you out of all trouble.

And, oh, what a glorious deliverance awaits the believer from out the depths of the grave on the morning of the first resurrection, when the trump of Jesus will wake all them who sleep in

Him. "Awake and sing, you that dwell in dust: for your dew is as the dew of herbs, and the earth shall cast out the dead." Such is the resurrection-song which will float in its sweetest cadence over the grave- penetrating its deepest recesses, and waking its profoundest slumber- of all who departed this life in Christ's faith and fear.

In view of the believer's present deliverance from the body of sin, suffering and death, and in anticipation of his future deliverance from the pit of corruption, with a body molded like unto Christ's glorious body- no more sin, no more sickness, no more sorrow, no more death, no more separations- may we not join with the deepest gratitude of our hearts in the beautiful thanksgiving which we pronounce over the holy dead: "Almighty God, with whom do live the spirits of those who depart hence in the Lord, and with whom the souls of the faithful, after they are delivered from the burden of the flesh, are in joy and felicity: let it please You, of your gracious goodness, shortly to accomplish the number of Your elect, and to hasten Your kingdom; that we, with all those that are departed in the true faith of Your holy name, may have our perfect consummation and bliss, both in body and soul, in Your eternal and everlasting glory; through Jesus Christ our Lord."

Out of the depths I cry,
Oppressed with grief and sin;
O gracious Lord, draw nigh,
Complete Your work within.
O listen to Your suppliant's voice,
And let my broken bones rejoice.
'Out of the depths I cried,
Overwhelmed with wrath divine,'
Said Christ, when crucified
For guilty souls like mine:
His cries were heard-He died,
and rose Triumphant over all His foes.

Prayer Out of Soul Depths

"Out of the depths have I cried unto You, O Lord. Lord, hear my voice: let your ears be attentive to the voice of my supplications." Psalm 130:1-2.

Seasons of soul-depths are ever seasons of heart-prayer in the Christian's experience. At no period does the divine life of the regenerate so strongly and triumphantly vindicate its nature, and assert its reality and power, as then. This was the case under consideration. "Out of the depths have I cried unto you, O Lord." That must indeed be a "depth," a soundless depth of spiritual despondency, in which the soul is either debarred from prayer, or is so imprisoned, that it cannot send up its cries to God. But this was not the case of David. He gave himself immediately and unreservedly to prayer. "I cried unto you, O Lord."

What irrefragable evidence he affords of the existence of that spiritual life in the living soul which cannot die; of that faith in the believing soul which cannot be repressed; of that divine love in the loving soul which many waters cannot quench! Communion with God is the outbreathing of the quickened soul, and no distance can arrest, or condition stifle it.

"From the end of the earth will I cry unto you, when my heart is overwhelmed." Deep exercise of soul is often God's mode of rousing the slumbering spirit, and quickening the sluggish energy of prayer. Its potency and pre-eminence are only learned to any great extent when faith is tried, and the heart is overwhelmed, and the soul is plunged into great "depths." But, sink the soul as it may, the arrow of prayer, feathered with a divine promise, springing from the bow of faith, and winged by the power of the Spirit will overcome every obstacle, pierce every cloud, and fasten itself upon the throne of the Eternal God!

Was not this the experience of Jonah? "I cried by reason of my affliction unto the Lord, and He heard me; out of the belly of hell (his watery grave) cried I, and you heard me." But a greater than Jonah shall testify. Were there ever such fathomless soul depths as Christ's, when, as their Divine substitute, He bore their sins, endured their curse, and suffered the wrath of God on behalf of His people? "Save me, O God; for the waters are come in unto my soul. I sink in deep mire, where there is no standing." Behold, He prays! And as He advanced into the tornado of the curse, the storm thickening and darkening around Him- as He sank deeper and yet deeper into the mountain billows of divine wrath- the huge breakers surging and foaming around His holy soul- as He exhausted drop by drop 'the cup of trembling,' until the very lees touched His quivering lips, lo! "He Prayed More Earnestly!" The intensity of His prayer rose with the agony of His spirit; its earnestness gathered strength with the anguish of His soul. "Being in an agony He Prayed More Earnestly."

Sinking, suffering saint, learn the secret of your support! "He prayed more earnestly." "Who in the days of His flesh, when He offered up prayers and supplications with strong crying and tears unto Him that was able to save Him from death, and was heard in that He feared." Go you and do likewise. Pray- pray- PRAY! Out of the depths of your difficulty, your need, your sorrow, cry mightily unto God. There is no 'depth' so profound, no darkness so dense, no need so pressing, or perplexity so great, but from it you may cry unto God, the Lord inclining His ear to the softest, faintest breathing of your soul. "For this shall every one that is godly pray unto you in a time when you may be found: surely in the floods of great waters they shall not come near unto him." Cries out of the depths of soul-distress have a peculiar eloquence and an irresistible success with God just as the plaintive wail of a sick and suffering child reaches and penetrates a parent's heart more quickly and more deeply than all others. It is a beautiful thought embodied in the Psalmist's prayer: "My soul hangs upon God. "

Look for a moment at the Object upon which the believing, sinking soul thus hangs. It is upon DEITY. The world around is hanging upon every object but God. Some are hanging upon self, some upon their wealth- some upon their intellectual powers-some upon their bodily strength-some upon their long life- some upon the creature- some upon their own righteousness; all are hanging upon some object below Christ and God. How frail and fatal the support! Soon the prop bends- the stirrup breaks- the fulcrum yields- the sands glide away- and great is the fall of him who suspended upon such created and fragile support his happiness in this life, and his hope of the life that is to come.

But, the believing soul, though a desponding and sinking soul, hangs upon GOD. Listen to the language of David: "O God, you are my God; early will I seek you: my soul thirsts for you, my flesh longs for you in a dry and thirsty land, where no water is." Again: "Whom have I in heaven but You? and there is none upon earth that I desire beside You." This is the support of every gracious soul; and he who hangs not upon this divine support, hangs upon air, hangs upon nothing.

Listen to Jehoshaphat's prayer in his distress, when the mighty hosts of the Ammonites came against him to battle. See how he hung upon God! "O our God, will you not judge them? for we have no might against this great company that comes against us; neither know we what to do: our eyes are upon You. " And the Lord delivered them into his hand that day, and all that he did was to stand still and see the salvation of the Lord. And thus was it with Asa. Oppressed by a powerful enemy, too strong for his scanty forces, he thus hung upon God in his extremity. "Lord, it is nothing with you to help, whether with many, or with those who have no power." And what a "nail in a sure place" is the Lord Jesus Christ, the true, spiritual Eliakim, upon whom the soul may hang its sins, and sorrows, and hope of glory. "I will fasten him," says the Father, "as a nail in a sure place. . . And they shall hang upon him all the glory of his father's house .... all the vessels."

Sin-burdened soul, sinking into depths of guilt and despair, come; and hang in faith upon this Divine, this most sure nail, and you shall be saved! Hang upon Him as a personal Savior! Hang upon His blood to cleanse, upon His righteousness to justify, upon His grace to subdue, upon His fullness to supply, upon His willingness and power to save you to the uttermost extent of your sin and guilt. Hang upon God upon His strength to deliver you, upon His wisdom to counsel you, upon His love to comfort you, upon His infinite resources to meet your every need; and your song shall be,

"Other refuge have I none,

HANGS my helpless soul ON YOU."

Oh give yourself to prayer! If words fail you- if by reason of the anguish of your spirit there is no outlet for your feelings but in the plaintive language of sighs and groans and tears -still uplift your soul to God in mental supplication and heart breathing, and your testimony shall be that of David: "The Lord has heard the voice of my weeping." "Lord, all my desire is before You; and my groaning is not hid from You." And thus, when by reason of the anguish of your spirit, the cloud-veil of your mind, and the infirmity of your body, you can neither think nor pray, let the reflection cheer you that Jesus is thinking of, and praying for, you. "When I cannot think of Jesus," said a sick one whom He loved, "Jesus is thinking of me." Happy thought!

It is a truth fraught with the richest comfort that, sink the tried and desponding soul as it may, it can never sink below the everlasting arms of God. God is frequently wont to permit His children to descend into great "depths" of spiritual and mental conflict, and even temporal need, that He might display His love and power in stooping to their necessity. "I was brought low, and He helped me." "Bow down your ear to me; deliver me speedily: be my strong rock, for a house of defense to save me."

We are but imperfectly aware how low the great God can bend to our case- how condescendingly Christ can stoop to our condition! We may be brought very low- our case sad and desperate: riches may flee; poverty may come upon us as an armed man; character may be assailed; children may try; friends may change; enemies may wound; death may bereave; and our soul be plunged as into fathomless depths. Nevertheless, sink deep as we may, we shall but sink more deeply into the embrace of Christ, 'the everlasting arms' still underneath us. "He sent from above, He took me; He drew me out of many waters." Oh we must descend into great depths of affliction, of trial, and of need, to fathom, in some measure, the soundless depths of God's love, of the Savior's fullness, of the Spirit's comfort!

And still our strong refuge is prayer- prayer in all depths. "Out of the depths have I cried unto You, O Lord." "From the end of the earth will I cry unto You, when my heart is overwhelmed." Oh, give yourself to prayer! No difficulty is too great, no trial too severe, to take to Jesus. If your sins and guilt appear to you a depth so abysmal that no line could fathom it, remember that God's mercy in Christ Jesus is infinite; that, if there are great depths in your sinfulness and unworthiness, there are infinitely greater depths in the sin-forgiving love of God, in the sin-atoning blood and sinner-justifying righteousness of the Redeemer.

Sunk though you are in sin, steeped in crime and guilt, countless and great your departures from God, your rejection of the Savior, your religious unbelief, stifled convictions, and scarred conscience; nevertheless, you have not sunk below the depths of God's love and of Christ's grace. The prodigal had wandered far from his father, he had sunk into great depths of poverty and degradation and need; yet, when he 'came to himself' he exclaimed, "I will arise and go to my father, and will say unto him, Father, I have sinned; and his father saw him a great way off, and had compassion, and ran, and embraced him." That Father is your heavenly Father, and waits to enfold you to His loving and forgiving heart!

Depth of mercy! can there be

Mercy still reserved for me?
Can my God His wrath forbear,
Me, the chief of sinners, spare?
I have long withstood His grace,
Long provoked Him to His face;
Would not hearken to His calls,
Grieved Him by a thousand falls.
　JESUS, answer from above,
Is not all Your nature love?
Will You not the wrong forget?
Suffer me to kiss Your feet?
If I rightly read Your heart,
If You all compassion art,
Now Your ear in mercy bow,
Pardon and accept me now."

But, prayer is necessary, not only when in our depths, but to be preserved from them. And to prayer must be united sleepless vigilance. "Watch and pray," is our Lord's twofold injunction, given on the most impressive occasion and amid the most affecting circumstances of His life. The calling of a child of God is high and holy. It is all the more essential that he should walk carefully, watchfully, and prayerfully, lest his feet slide; and thus, losing his steadfastness in the faith and his close communion with God, he fall into "the depths of Satan," the seductions of the flesh, and the allurements of the world; and so plunging into 'depths' of doubt, darkness, and despondency.

The path of spiritual declension is an 'sloped plane', each step accelerating the rapidity of the soul's descent. It commences at the closet. The restraining of prayer- especially private devotion-
is the first stage in the decay and declension of the believer in the divine life. Soon will follow the fascination and power of the world; and when the world enters like a flood, Christ and prayer and eternal realities are swept before its impetuous torrent, then the gracious soul is stranded upon the bleak, rock-bound coast of bitter remorse and dark despair.

What an appalling picture does the inspired penman draw of the final condition of the unregenerate apostate from his profession of Christ and the faith! "It is impossible for those who were once enlightened, and have tasted of the heavenly gift, and were made partakers of the Holy Spirit, and have tasted the good word of God, and the powers of the world to come, if they shall fall away, to renew them again unto repentance; seeing they crucify to themselves the Son of God afresh, and put Him to an open shame." Whatever interpretation these awful declarations will admit- and to the truly regenerate they cannot by any ingenuity of criticism, or justness of exegesis, properly apply, since a true child of God, though he may sadly backslide, and be sorely chastened, cannot finally perish- they yet are words of solemn significance, well calculated to fill the soul of the Christian professor, and even the true believer, with holy trembling, rousing him to the imperious and difficult task of unswerving self-vigilance and unwearied prayer.

The present chapter speaks pointedly and solemnly to the unconverted reader. There is beyond this present life a "depth" awfully and significantly termed "the bottomless pit." It is the final and eternal doom of all who die out of Christ. It is immeasurable and soundless. No line of grace can fathom it, no arm of mercy can reach it, no voice of love ever wakes its echoes, and eternity alone will see the end of its woe. "These shall go away into everlasting punishment." "The wicked shall be turned into hell."

But, is there no escape from a final and eternal doom so appalling? Listen to the voice of divine love. "Save him from going down to the pit; I have found a ransom!" That ransom is the atoning blood of Jesus, and He the sinner's Ransomer. Escape for your life! Look not behind; but in faith hasten to Christ, the City of Refuge, and you shall be saved from the wrath that is to come! Oh, blessed thought! No poor awakened sinner ever betook himself to that Divine refuge and found the door closed against him. "Believe on the Lord Jesus Christ, and you shall be saved."

Soon the soul-desponding saint will ascend from the lowest depths of earth to the loftiest height of heaven. Long before the body springs from the dust, your soul, O believer, will have taken its place amid the blood-ransomed throng, clustering in shining ranks around the throne of God and the Lamb. And, reviewing all the way the Lord your God led you, through the wilderness and across the desert, you shall blend the old song of free grace with the new song of eternal glory, and exclaim,

"I waited patiently for the Lord; and he inclined unto me, and heard my cry. He brought me up also out of an horrible pit, out of the miry clay, and set my feet upon a rock, and established my goings. And he has put a new song in my mouth, even praise unto our God."

"PARDON, my Master, pardon for my weakness,Thus shrinking, fainting, beneath my Father's rod; Oh, grant to me Your pure and patient meekness! Sincerely would I say, 'No will but Yours, O God.'

"Even as a reed by the rough tempest shivered,
Trembling I bend before Your chastening breath,
And low within my heart faith's flame has quivered,
Until all seemed shadowed like the vale of death.

"I strive to walk the stormy wave, upheaving
Its angry might, but sink wherever I tread;
I know Your covenant sure, but scarce believing,
Still hangs upon my breast my aching head.

"Your promises like countless stars are shining:I see them not; for the clouds the heavens obscure!

I wrestle hard against each vain repining,And fear to murmur when I would endure.

"Come to my help, O Master! once in sorrow,
My more than brother, King of glory now;
Even in my tears a gleam of hope I borrow
From the deep scars around Your radiant brow.

"Come to my help, as once God's angels hastened
To cheer You in Your midnight agony;
O Lord of angels, by man's suffering chastened,
Forget not I am dust, infirmity.
"Come to me quickly, even as You have spoken
Your faithful word. Let me but hear Your voice;
Say You are with me, and the heart all broken
Again with holy gladness shall rejoice.
"Now round the 'bruised reed' Your grace enwreathing,
Upward to heaven once more I shall aspire;
Now on my darkened soul Your Spirit breathing,
Brightly shall flame again the failing fire.
"Walk You the wave with me, the tempest stilling;
Let me but feel the clasping of Your strength,
Your righteous strength, through all my pulses thrilling;
Nor shall I fear to reach the shore at length.
"Beam forth, O Morning Star, in mercy glorious,
With Your day-promise, from the troubled sky;
Hold forth the fadeless crown, and palm victorious,
You who have fought and won, to cheer my eye.
"What means that strain, sweeter than angels' singing?
Oh, can it be Your own responsive word,
Mysterious music on my senses ringing
'Fear not, you trembler; for your prayer is heard'?

Contrition and Confession

"If You, Lord, should mark iniquities, O Lord, who shall stand?" Psalm cxxx. 3.

It is said, and we believe with truth, that, to the eye of the miner, entombed deep in the heart of the earth, the heavens appear at noonday studded with myriads of the most brilliant planets, invisible at the same moment from the earth's surface. The phenomenon is easy of solution. It is night with the miner, in his depths; and the darkest night reveals wonders and splendors which the brightest day conceals. May not this simple fact furnish an apt illustration of our present subject? Some of the most glorious unfoldings of God's character and of Christ's beauty, of divine truth and lessons of the Christian life, are found in those 'soul-depths' we have been describing, not always experienced by believers who, for the most part, dwell but upon the surface of the divine life.

Not the least important is the subject of our present chapter- the holiness of God, and the contrition and confession of the believer. "If You, Lord, should mark iniquities, O Lord, who shall stand?" To the consideration of these points let us address ourselves, as the Holy Spirit shall aid us. The subject is solemn and important- the most solemn and important of all subjects. Right and deep views of sin lie at the root of correct and high views of God; and low thoughts of God inevitably engender low perceptions of sin.

Dr. Owen, in his instructive Exposition of this Psalm, though somewhat verbose, thus forcibly puts the matter: "The generality of men make light work of sin; and yet in nothing does it more appear what thoughts they have of God. He that has light thoughts of sin had never great thoughts of God. Indeed, men's underrating of sin arises merely from their contempt of God. All sin's concernments place its relation unto God. And as men's conceptions are of God, so will they be of sin, which is an opposition to Him. This is the frame of the most of men; they know little of God, and are little troubled about anything that relates unto Him. God is not reverenced; sin is but a trifle; forgiveness a matter of nothing; whosoever will may have it for nothing. But shall the atheistical wickedness of the heart of man be called a discovery of forgiveness? Is not this to make God an idol? He who is not acquainted with God's holiness and purity, who knows not sin's deceit and sinfulness, knows nothing of forgiveness." The groundwork, then, of our present subject is, the essential holiness of God, upon which is based the soul's godly sorrow for sin. To these solemn points let us direct our devout attention.

The highest and most glorious perfection of God is His essential HOLINESS. He would cease to be God could He cease to be holy, holiness being, not an accident, but an intrinsic perfection of His Being. It is the uniting bond of all His other perfections, imparting existence, cohesion, and beauty to all. "The nature of God cannot rationally be conceived without it. Though the power of God be the first rational conclusion drawn from the light of His works and wisdom, the next from the order and connection of His works, purity must result from the beauty of His works. God cannot be deformed by evil who has made everything so beautiful in His time. The notion of a God cannot be entertained without separating from Him whatever is impure and bespotting, both in His essence and actions. Though we conceive Him infinite in majesty, infinite in essence, eternal in duration, mighty in power, and wise and immutable in His counsels, merciful in His proceedings with men, and whatever other perfections may dignify so sovereign a Being: yet if we conceive Him destitute of these excellent perfections, and imagine Him possessed with the least contagion of evil; we make Him but an infinite monster, and sully all these perfections we ascribed to Him before; we rather own Him a devil than a God. It is a less injury to Him to deny His Being than to deny the purity of it. The one makes Him no God, the other deformed, unholy, and detestable." (Charnock)

God is declared to be "glorious in holiness;" so holy that it is said "He cannot look upon sin;" that is, cannot look upon it but with infinite hatred and abhorrence. "You are of purer eyes than to behold evil, and can not look on iniquity." He swears by His holiness. "Once have I sworn by my holiness, that I will not lie unto David." "The Lord will swear by His holiness." Holiness, as we have remarked, is the luster and beauty of His Being. "How great is His beauty," because how perfect is His holiness! "Power is His arm; omniscience, His eye; mercy, His heart; eternity, His duration; HOLINESS, His BEAUTY." "The beauty of holiness."

Passing over the many exceptional proofs God has given of His hatred of sin, and His solemn determination to punish it- for example, the destruction of the old world by water, and that of the cities of the plain by fire; let us bend our thoughts to the most significant and appalling demonstration of His holiness the universe ever beheld, infinitely distancing and transcending every other- the sufferings and death of His only and beloved Son. The cross of Calvary exhibits God's hatred and punishment of sin in a way and to an extent which the annihilation of millions of worlds, swept from the face of the universe by the broom of His wrath, could never have done.

The Surety and Substitute of His elect Church; bearing her sins, and exhausting her curse-divine law and justice exacted from Him the utmost equivalent; the one, a perfect obedience, the other, the penalty of death. "Christ was once offered to bear the sins of many." "Who His own self bore our sins in His own body on the tree." "He was wounded for our transgressions, He was bruised for our iniquities." In all this we beheld a most awful display of God's hatred of sin. Finding the sins of the Church upon Christ as its Surety, Substitute, and Savior, the wrath of God was poured out upon Him without measure! To what other rational cause can we ascribe the profound emotion which these words describe: "My soul is sorrowful, even unto death." "And being in an agony .... He sweat great drops of blood, falling down to the ground." "My Father, if it be possible, let this cup pass from me"? He had never transgressed. "Holy, harmless, and undefiled," He was free from every taint of sin.

Jesus had never broken God's law; but, on the contrary, "had done always those things which pleased Him." And yet, pure and obedient though He was, God finding the sins of His people laid upon His Son, emptied upon His holy soul all the vials of His wrath due to their transgressions. Go, my soul, to Calvary, and learn how holy God is, and what a monstrous thing sin is, and how imperiously, solemnly, and holily bound Jehovah is to punish it, either in the person of the sinner, or in the person of a Surety.

Could the personal sinlessness of Christ exempt Him from this terrible punishment? Could it in any measure lessen or mitigate the tremendous infliction of God the Father's wrath? Impossible! It was not Christ who was penally punished: it was the sins of His elect Church, which He voluntarily and fully bore, punished in Him. Never was the Son of God dearer to the Father than at the very moment that the sword of divine justice, flaming and flashing, pierced to its hilt His holy heart. But it was the wrath of God, not against His beloved Son, but against the sins which met on Him when presenting Himself on the cross as the substitutionary sacrifice and offering of His Church. He "gave Himself for us." What a new conception must angels have formed of the exceeding sinfulness of sin, when they beheld the flaming sword of justice quenched in the holy, loving bosom of Jesus! And in what a dazzling light does this fact place the marvellous love of God to sinners! Man's sin and God's love- the indescribable enormity of the one, and the immeasurable greatness of the other- are exhibited in the cross of Christ as nowhere else. Oh to learn experimentally these two great facts- sin's infinite hatefulness, and love's infinite holiness! The love of God in giving His Son to die; the love of Christ in dying; the essential turpitude and unmitigated enormity of SIN, which demanded a sacrifice so Divine, so holy, and so precious!

On the wings of faith uprising,
Jesus crucified I see;
While His love, my soul surprising,
Cries, 'I suffered all for thee.
Then, beneath the cross adoring,
Sin cloth like itself appear,
When the wounds of Christ exploring,
I can read my pardon there.
Angels here may gaze and wonder
What the God of love could mean,
When that heart was torn asunder,
Never once defiled with sin.

Nor this alone. In the cross of Christ we not only see the enormity of man's sin and the greatness of God's love, but in the Atonement there offered the believing soul beholds the entire cancelling of all his transgressions, the complete blotting out of the thick cloud of all his guilt. Viewed in this light, as a penitent believer, you have nothing, in the sense of propitiation, to do with your sins. The work of propitiation is all done by Christ your Surety. "Whom God has set forth to be a propitiation for our sins;" and when this was done, "there remains no more sacrifice for sins," Christ's one offering of Himself has forever perfected those who are sanctified. Cease, then, to look upon the great debt as though Jesus had not discharged it; upon the mighty bond; as though He had not cancelled it; upon your countless sins, as though His blood had not washed them all away.

You have nothing to do with your sins- past, present, or to come- but to mortify the root, to combat vigorously their ascendancy, and to wash constantly in the divine laver of Christ's atoning blood, confessing daily and hourly sins, with the hand of faith laid upon the head of the sacrificial Lamb thus walking as before God with a quickened, tender, purified conscience, desiring in all things to please Him.

"If You, Lord, should mark iniquities, O Lord, who shall stand?" CONTRITION is the first feeling in David's experience which these words indicate. It was in the "depths" that this most holy grace was inspired. The believer has need to be brought into a very close knowledge of himself to learn what true and deep contrition for sin is. The deepest humiliation, the warmest tears, the most broken and contrite spirit, are not often found in the 'high places' where the soul is privileged to walk. We must descend from the mount into the valley, and in the valley "lie low in a low place" yes, the lowest; to learn the meaning and force of David's prayer: "O Lord, pardon mine iniquity; for it is great;" and of Job's acknowledgment: "I abhor myself, and repent in dust and ashes."

Oh, what a volume of meaning do these words contain, as they apply to our individual selves: "If You, Lord, should mark iniquities," my iniquities- the depravity of my nature, the sinfulness of my heart, the unrighteousness of my most holy things- my thoughts and imaginations, my words and actions, my covetousness, worldliness, and carnality; my low aims, selfish motives, and by-ends; O Lord, how could I stand? In this light we must interpret David's contrite words; and thus interpreted, with what solemnity and self-application will they come home to every bosom in which throbs one pulse of spiritual life- in which glows one spark of divine love!

Cultivate, beloved, a holy contrition for sin. Subject your heart to the closest anatomy, your actions to the most searching analysis, your mental conceptions, motives, and words, to the most rigid and faithful scrutiny. This godly sorrow, and holy contrition, will preserve your heart pure and tender, your spirit lowly and watchful, your holy posture and place ever low beneath the cross.

An old divine thus appropriately discourses: "The merchant never allows a single day to elapse without taking an account of what he may have gained or lost in the course of it: let us do the same by our souls. Let not one evening pass over our heads without our examining how our spiritual account stands; let us enter into the inmost recesses of our heart, and ask ourselves, "In what have I offended God during the day? Have I indulged in idle conversation? Have I sinned by neglecting to perform my duties? Have I tried too hardly the patience of any of my debtors? Have I tried too hardly the patience of any of my brethren? Have I injured the reputation of any one by my words? When I have seemed to take part in holy things, has not my mind been occupied with the affairs of this world? When the concupiscence of the flesh has presented its dangerous poisons to me, have I not voluntarily inclined my lips towards the cup? And under whatever of these or other heads we may find ourselves on the debtor side, let us lament over our transgressions from our inmost souls, and labor to make up tomorrow what we may have lost today."

The effect of this holy scrutiny will be humble contrition, and that in its turn will be exceedingly bitter; nevertheless, the more bitter our repentance, the sweeter the fruit. It is said by naturalists that the bitterest flower yields the sweetest honey. Bitter in their bud, fruits gain sweetness as they advance to maturity; so it is with the exercises of penitence- they begin by being bitter, but they end by growing sweet.

Hence our dear Lord said, "Blessed are those who weep." What! are tears blessed? Is weeping sweet? Yes! Not the tears falling upon the coffin and the grave of loved ones of whom death has bereaved us; not the tears wept over ruined fortune, and lowered circumstances, and alienated friendship; but, blessed are they who weep over their sins, lament their backslidings, and mourn their spiritual lapses and wilful wanderings from the strait and narrow road to heaven, as beneath the shadow of the cross.

CONFESSION is another element of David's acknowledgment. "If You, Lord, should mark iniquities, O Lord, who shall stand?" These words involve a personal and humble acknowledgment of sin on the part of the psalmist. Confession of sin is a consequence of contrition for sin. No grace in the 'royal penitent' was more conspicuous than the grace of confession to God. "I acknowledged my sin unto You, and my iniquity have I not hid. I said, I will confess my transgressions unto the Lord." "I acknowledge my transgressions: and my sin is ever before me."

And here we touch upon a duty- no, a privilege- the most holy, spiritual, and sanctifying of the Christian life- confession of sin to God. What a significant and magnificent confession have we in these words: "If You, Lord, should mark iniquities, O Lord, who shall stand?" We cannot urge upon the reader a more spiritual, purifying, and comforting habit than this. It seems to involve every spiritual grace of the Christian character; an intelligent apprehension of sin, sincere repentance, deep humiliation, living faith, holy love, and a simple turning of the soul to Jesus.

Why is it that so many of God's saints travel all their days with their heads bowed like a bulrush? Why so few attain to the high standard of an assured interest in Christ? Why so many walk in the spirit of legal bondage, knowing little or nothing of their pardon, adoption, and acceptance? May it not, to a great degree, be traced to their lax habit of confession of sin to God? It is because they go day by day, and week by week, bearing along their lonely, dusty road, the burden of conscious sin and uncleansed guilt. Oh, the great secret of a pure, holy, and happy walk is in living close by God's confessional- is in going with the slightest aberration of the mind, with the faintest consciousness of guilt, and at once, with the eye upon the blood, unveiling and acknowledging it, without the slightest concealment or mental reservation, to God! So long as this holy privilege is neglected, guilt, like a corroding poison, an inflamed wound, a festering sore, eats as a canker into the very vitals of our peace and joy and hope.

This was David's testimony: "When I kept silence, my bones waxed old through my roaring all the day long. For day and night your hand was heavy upon me: my moisture is turned into the drought of summer. I acknowledged my sin unto You, and my iniquity have I not hid. I said, I will confess my transgressions unto the Lord; and You forgave the iniquity of my sin."

Do not suppose that, because contrition and confession were among the earliest exercises of your conversion, that there they ended. God forbid! They belong to each stage, and should trace every step of the Christian life. The close of that life is often marked by the deepest, holiest, and most evangelical sorrow for sin; the dying eye moistened with contrition's last and latest and most precious tear. What most endears the open Fountain? What leads us the most frequently and the most believingly to bathe in its ever-fresh, ever-flowing, ever-cleansing stream? What makes Jesus so precious? Oh, it is the daily, the constant habit of confession. We must ever remember that the Paschal Lamb was eaten with bitter herbs, and that those bitter herbs imparted a sweetness to the sacrificial offering. And thus it is that, the bitter herbs of repentance, blended with a holy confession of sin at the cross, imparts a higher estimation of the Atonement, an additional sweetness to the blood, and renders the Savior more precious to the heart. Oh the peace, the repose, the light, which springs from the confession of sin to God, no imagination can conceive or words express!

A simple personal incident may illustrate the idea. Sauntering on one occasion through the 'long-drawn aisles' of a Roman Catholic Cathedral, my eye was arrested by one of the numerous dreary-looking "confessionals" which invariably obtrude from the walls of those foreign edifices. While musing upon the object, a young female in modest attire approached, and, prostrating herself at the feet of the ghostly priest, placed her mouth close to his ear as he bent his head to receive her confession. In a short time she arose, and with a flushed countenance, a beaming eye, and an air of conscious relief, passed me quickly on her way. She had unveiled the sacred, and perhaps guilty, secrets of her

heart to the ear of the ghostly confessor, had received his "absolution," and retired from the church with the aspect of one from off whose soul a terrible weight of sin and terror had been removed. And, as in solemn reflection I gazed upon the melancholy spectacle, I thought If such the soul-peace, such the mental relief, which confession to a poor sinful mortal induces-false though it be; what must be the divine, what the true repose and comfort of a humble, penitential, and unreserved confession of sin to God, through Christ Jesus!

Christian do not carry the burden of your sin a single step further; the moment the consciousness of guilt and departure from God oppresses you, however apparently slight it may appear- a thought, a look, a passion, a word, an act- repair immediately to the feet of Jesus, disclose it without the slightest mental reservation, and, by a renewed application of atoning blood, seek its immediate and entire removal. Thus penitentially confessing and divinely absolved, you shall uprise from the feet of the great High Priest, exclaiming, with a lightened conscience and a praiseful heart, "I acknowledged my sin unto You, and my iniquity have I not hid. I said, I will confess my transgressions unto the Lord; and You forgave the iniquity of my sin."

"If You, Lord, should mark iniquities, O Lord, who shall stand?" The false and fatal idea of the ungodly is, that God does not "mark" -that is, does not notice or record "iniquity" -forgetting the solemn declarations of His own word: "The ways of man are before the eyes of the Lord, and He ponders all his goings." "The eyes of the Lord are in every place, beholding the evil and the good." Oh that these weighty declarations may sink deep into our hearts! The most holy saint of God needs them.

If the Lord should mark, ponder, chasten the iniquity of our most holy things- the double motive, the self-seeking end, the sinful infirmity, which attaches to our best and holiest doings, who of us could stand in His presence? All that we do for God, and for Christ, and for our fellows, is deformed and tainted by human infirmity and sin. A close scrutiny and analysis of our most saintly act would discover the leprosy of iniquity deeply hidden beneath its apparent loveliness and sanctity. How humbling, yet how true! We have need to weep over our tears, to repent of our

repentances, to confess our confessions; and, when our most fervent prayer has been breathed, and our most self-denying act has been performed, and our most liberal offering has been presented, and our most powerful sermon has been preached, and our sweetest anthem has poured forth its music, we have need to repair to the "blood that cleanses from ALL sin," even the sins of our most holy things!

How instructive and impressive the type! "You shall make a plate of pure gold, and grave upon it, like the engravings of a signet, HOLINESS TO THE LORD.... And it shall be upon Aaron's forehead, that Aaron may bear the iniquity of the holy things, which the children of Israel shall hallow in all their holy gifts; and it shall be always upon his forehead, that they may be accepted before the Lord." Thus has Christ, our true Aaron, made a full Atonement for the "iniquity of our holy things;" and the mitre is always upon His head, that our persons and our offerings may be ever accepted before the Lord.

This brings us to the answer which the Gospel supplies to the searching, solemn question: "If You, Lord, should mark iniquity, who shall stand?" The Gospel reveals Christ as the Great Sin-Bearer of the sinner, and this is the answer of faith to the solemn, searching challenge. We can do nothing in the way of penitence, confession, and forgiveness until we see all our sins and iniquities- both those of our unconverted, and those of our converted life- laid upon Jesus. We must see Him "wounded for our transgressions, and bruised for our iniquities." We must see Him who knew no sin made a sin-offering for us; our sins put upon Christ, and, in return, His righteousness put upon us; Christ and the sinner thus changing places, the One assuming the sin, and the other receiving the righteousness. "For He has made Him to be sin for us, who knew no sin; that we might be made the righteousness of God in Him." And now, when the question returns with personal force, "Should God mark my iniquities, how can I stand?" let faith, resting upon the divine word, answer, "Jesus is my Substitute: Jesus stood in my place: Jesus bore my sins: Jesus did all, suffered all, and paid all in my stead, and here I rest." Oh, yes, the believing sinner, robed with the righteousness of Christ, stands now before the holy Lord God, freely and completely justified from all things; and will stand in the great day of the Lord without spot or wrinkle, when the heavens and the earth are fleeing before His face, and when the wicked are calling upon the rocks and the mountains to fall upon them, and hide them from the wrath of the Lamb; for the great day of His wrath will have come, and who shall be able to stand?"When from the dust of death I rise to take my mansion in the skies, Even then shall this be all my plea, Jesus has lived and died for me." Bold shall I stand in that great day; For who aught to my charge shall lay? While through Your blood absolved I am from sin's tremendous curse and shame."

Forgiveness and Fear

"But there is forgiveness with You, that You may be feared." Psalm 130:4.

The exercise of pardon is the exclusive and the highest prerogative of the crown, the richest and most brilliant gem in the diadem of an earthly Sovereign. This applies to God. It is no marvel, then, that He-the sin-pardoning God, should have guarded this, His divine right and most gracious act, with a jealousy so great, and have linked it with conditions so solemn. "Who is a God like unto You, that pardons iniquity?" "There is forgiveness with You."

As pardon is God's most divine and gracious act, it follows, then, that we could know nothing of it but by revelation. No light of nature could disclose it, no effort of reason could discover it. It could not possibly be known by the research of man, and it must be exclusively revealed by the mercy of God. That God had the power of pardoning none could doubt; that power being supremely lodged in His hand, in whom the legislative, judicial, and executive authority of the universe met. But from what oracle in nature could we expect the announcement that God would exercise His prerogative of pardoning, and exercise it by a mode and with conditions the most stupendous and marvelous, such as could never have entered into the mind of angels or men to have conceived? All nature would be dumb. God, then, must be the Revealer of His power, will, and mode of pardoning. And how gloriously and clearly has He done it!

Recall the scene that appeared to Moses in the mount. "And the Lord descended in the cloud, and stood with him there, and proclaimed the name of the Lord. The Lord God, merciful and gracious, patient, and abundant in goodness and truth, keeping mercy for thousands, FORGIVING iniquity, transgression, and sin." Thus on the mount Sinai, amid its thunder, and fire, and smoke-emblems of His majesty and holiness- God revealed His character and purpose as a sin forgiving God.

We turn to mount Calvary, and amid its darkness and trembling- the sun draped in sackcloth, the earth quaking, the rocks rending- tokens of His grace and love- we learn the wonderful mode of His pardoning. "Who is a God like unto You, that PARDONS iniquity?" "There is FORGIVENESS with You." How priceless and precious to us should be that inspired volume which reveals this glorious fact, that there is forgiveness with God! How gratefully should we receive it, how firmly believe it, how valiantly defend it, and how zealously and generously diffuse it, sending it forth, borne upon the crest of every wave, and upon the wings of every wind, to the remotest limits of the earth. "The leaves of the tree were for the healing of the nations."

Aided by the power of contrast, we purpose, in the further unfolding of this subject, to place side by side man's forgiveness and God's; in other words, forgiveness as exercised by a human government, and forgiveness as exercised by a Divine government. Take the first point of contrast which forgiveness involves- honor to the law broken, and security to the government offended. The considerations which induce a human executive to pardon are totally different from those which move the Divine-and here God and man stand in marked and diametrical opposition one to the other. How great the contrast!

There is nothing in the pardon of a human government to sustain the majesty of law, and to meet the claims of equity. No attempt is made to harmonize the claims of righteousness with the pleadings of mercy; to reconcile the act of pardon with the demands of holiness. No atonement is made, no satisfaction is offered, no penalty is executed; the law is dishonored, justice is outraged, and the government from where the act emanates is weakened, and its authority lowered in the eyes of the nation; in a word, the criminal is pardoned, and the crime is condoned!

Contrast this with the Divine pardon of sin. God rests His plan of forgiveness upon a basis which magnifies the law, whose violation He pardons; which executes the sentence, while He remits the penalty; which strengthens the government and lends luster to its administration, while He spares the sinner who has ignored its authority and rebelled against its commands. God thus takes the matter of 'satisfaction of justice' in His own hands- assumes the responsibility, arranges the preliminaries, and bears the entire cost of the plan- a cost which the infinite resources of Deity alone could meet. It will at once be seen that the great problem of His moral government which He engaged to solve -and He solved it was, the harmony of the respective claims of justice and mercy, of pardon and holiness, the dignity of the offended government with the forgiveness of the offender. To adjust these conflicting interests, and to harmonize their jarring attributes, was the great work in which Deity embarked- a work in all respects worthy of God. Through the Incarnation of the Son of God, by the preceptive obedience of His life, and by the atoning sufferings of His death, He so completely magnified the Divine Law, and so fully satisfied Divine justice, as rendered it righteous and honorable on the part of God to pardon, justify, and save the vilest sinners. Thus clearly the Apostle puts this great truth: "In whom [Christ] we have redemption through His blood, the FORGIVENESS of sins, according to the riches of His grace." "For as by one man's disobedience many were made sinners, so by the OBEDIENCE of one shall many be made righteous." And now, the chief of sinners may approach boldly the throne of grace and obtain mercy, since he has not only mercy to appeal to, but the merits of Christ to plead. Justice is satisfied, while pardon is extended, and God's character suffers no dishonor; and His government no injury in forgiving and justifying the most unworthy. We plead a sacrifice all the more acceptable because it is another's; we bring a righteousness all the more worthy because not our own. If God should fail to accept us- and most justly might He refuse- yet He will not fail to accept Christ, who obeyed and suffered, died and rose again, in our stead; and all the more because it is His own plan and provision for pardoning and saving the very chief of sinners.

And what human government pardons the criminal at so vast a cost and so great a sacrifice to Himself as God does? The process is facile and quick. It is but a word, a signature, and the criminal is pardoned, and his life is spared. But, at what a cost and by what a sacrifice does God pardon the guilt of sin and justify the person of the sinner! He "spared not His own Son, but gave Him up for us all." "God so loved the world, that He gave His only begotten Son, that whosoever believes in Him should not perish, but have everlasting life." How vast the cost! How immeasurable the sacrifice! "Herein is love, not that we loved God, but that He loved us, and sent His Son to be the propitiation for our sins." It cost God the surrender of His own dear Son, sent into the world poor, despised, and insulted, and at last to endure on the cross the indescribable tortures of a condemned malefactor, the ignominious death of a Roman slave. "Who is a God like unto You?"

But at what a cost to Jesus Himself was our forgiveness procured! Oh, what human thought can conceive, what moral arithmetic compute it? It distances all imagination, defies all research. The stoop of His Deity to humanity- His assumption of our nature in its lowest form of poverty and lowliness; free from all moral taint, yet subjected to all physical evil; sinless, yet bearing sin; innocent, yet suffering as guilty; His Divine soul swimming in the ocean of infinite blessedness, His human soul bowed to the lowest dust in woe, "sorrowful even unto death." In a word, it cost Him the sacrifice of Himself- His last drop of blood, His last breath of life- to purchase for us the Divine forgiveness, which remits entirely all our sins, and cancels to the utmost and forever all our guilt. "You are bought with a price"-a price which Heaven alone could find, which Deity alone could pay. Oh the love the redeeming, dying love of Christ, which passes knowledge!

"What shall we pay the Eternal Son,
That left the Heavens of His abode,
And to this wretched earth came down,
To bring us wanderers back to God?
"It cost Him death to save our lives;
To buy our souls, it cost His own;
And all the unknown joys He gives
Were bought with agonies unknown.
"Our everlasting love is due
To Him who ransomed sinners lost,
And pitied rebels when He knew
The vast expense His love would cost."

Take another point of contrast- the moral effect of a human and Divine forgiveness. In nothing is the weakness of a human pardon more conspicuous than in this. The moral reformation of our criminals has long been a problem baffling the most astute philosopher and the most benevolent philanthropist. It is true that the modern 'Reformatory' is an institution resulting from an attempt to supply a solution of the perplexing problem; but the plan, which as yet contemplates but the juvenile portion of our criminal population, is still an experiment: the great mass of our released criminals remain unreached. In most cases the guilt-steeped and hardened criminal is pardoned, only to relapse more deeply into crime; is released, but to go forth with one hand bearing aloft the rescript of his pardon, and with the other repeating, under more aggravated circumstances, and in a form more appalling, the identical crime which the Sovereign had but just graciously remitted. Pardon has, in most cases, not only failed to weaken the force of his depravity, to reform his vicious life, and secure his loyal obedience, but has proved a stimulus to a bolder conception and a more awful commission of crime. We now turn to the Divine forgiveness of the sinner. In no case has God ever been disappointed in the moral effects of pardon in the sinners pardoned. To extend the full and free remission of sin to the soul is at once certainly and forever to receive that soul's willing and loving obedience to His law. The slave of sin has become His loving servant, and the rebel against His authority His obedient child. Never has God regretted the extension of His forgiveness to the vilest sinner. Not only has the grace of pardon conquered him, but the sweet, holy source of pardon has supplied him with motives to believe the most touching and irresistible. The softening, melting, sanctifying influence of the cross has dissolved the corrosive power of sin-so to speak-in the heart, which now beats more freely and throbs more intensely with life and love to God, to Christ and holiness. The grace of pardon has been attended not only with an emancipating, but also with subduing effect; it not only has cancelled the guilt, but it has conquered the power of sin; it has not only deposed, but it has slain the tyrant. With an eye moist with tears and beaming with love, the pardoned soul gazes upon the cross of Jesus, and exclaims, "How can I do this great wickedness and sin against such suffering, such forgiveness, such love?" "He will subdue our iniquities." "Who is a God like unto You?" Another and most important point of contrast, refers to the character of the sins and the number of sinners to whom the forgiveness of God extends. There is, and necessarily must be, a limit to the extension of pardon by the human sovereign, both as to the nature of the crime and the number of the criminals. The prerogative of mercy among men is extended with fear. There are some violations of the law so aggravated and enormous, some criminals of so desperate and incorrigible a character, that not only would justice be palpably outraged, but a serious injury would be inflicted upon the community, by the extension of mercy to such. A selection from a number of criminals is made, and the degree of mercy is graduated to the nature and guilt of the crime. Not so is it with the Divine government. God promises pardon to every sinner, and for every sin, but this only on condition of sincere repentance, humble acknowledgment, and true faith in Christ Jesus. 'All manner of sin shall be forgiven unto men." For this marvellous, boundless display of His forgiving mercy He has made ample provision in the Person and work of His only and beloved Son. The Atonement of the Incarnate God, the righteous obedience of His life, and the sacrificial nature of His death, have not only made a way for the outflow of His mercy to the chief of sinners, but have rendered it infinitely just and holy on the part of God to pardon iniquity, transgression, and sin of the deepest hue of guilt, and more countless in number than the stars. "Come now, and let us reason together, says the Lord: though your sins be as scarlet, they shall be as white as snow; though they be red like crimson, they shall be as wool." Again, what earthly sovereign ever pardoned the criminal at such an expense to himself as God does? What would be thought of a proposal issuing from the Government that the Queen of the realm, in order to extend her royal clemency to the greatest felon that ever stood at the bar, should take one of her offspring-perhaps her only son whom she loved- and sacrifice him as a substitute to the majesty of the law, and as a satisfaction to the requirements of justice? Would not a proposal so unparalleled, so unheard of and astounding, awake throughout the nation the deepest and loudest echoes of execration and dismay? Would not the nation a thousand times prefer that the criminal should go free, and that law and justice be trodden in the dust, rather than that the royal mercy should be extended on such terms, and be bought at such a price? And yet

God- the sin-pardoning, sinner-saving God, has done all this! The language of inspiration can alone justify this stupendous truth. Listen to the astounding declaration! "God so loved the world, that He gave His only begotten Son, that whosoever believes in Him should not perish, but have everlasting life." "Herein is love, not that we loved God, but that He loved us, and sent His Son to be the propitiation for our sins." "Christ died for the ungodly." "He spared not His own Son, but gave Him up for us all." What more can we add? Is not this enough to vindicate the character of God, to set forth His great love, and to assure the vilest sinner that "there is forgiveness with God" for every degree of sin and for every contrite sinner- for every species of crime and for every penitent criminal?

Yet another point of contrast. What would be the nation's thought of the goodness and grace of the sovereign who, to the royal act of pardon, should bestow upon the criminal the noblest relation and the richest estate? And yet the sin-forgiving God does all this to the sinner whom He fully and freely pardons. He not only pardons, but justifies; not only justifies, but adopts, and with adoption confers upon His child "an inheritance incorruptible, undefiled, and that fades not away." "When the fulness of the time was come, God sent forth His Son, made of a woman, made under the law, to redeem those who were under the law, that we might receive the adoption of sons. And because you are sons, God has sent forth the Spirit of His Son into your hearts, crying, Abba, Father." Such is the divine relation, and such the heaven of glory, to which the forgiveness of God raises. If sin is pardoned, if the soul is justified, we stand in a relation to God nearer than angels, and shall occupy a mansion and a throne in heaven to which Gabriel himself might in vain aspire. "Who is a God like unto You, that pardons?"

But there remains a clause in this verse of the psalm pregnant with the deepest and holiest instruction: "There is forgiveness with You, that You may be FEARED." How can this be? exclaims the unreflecting mind. Fear, the fruit and effect of pardon! It is an incongruity- a paradox! And yet such is the word of God, and as such we believe and accept it. How, then, are we to interpret the clause? A holy, filial, loving fear of God is ever the effect of His full and free forgiveness of sin; it is the natural, spontaneous and blessed result. All fear, if apart from a sense of pardoned sin, is legal, servile, and slavish; it is not the fear of a forgiven sinner, of a pardoned child. The pardoned soul sees in the grace of the act, such a display of God's holiness and hatred of sin, such an unfolding of His grace and love, as at once inspires a holy, reverential, and child-like fear of offending Him. Never did the believing soul see sin's exceeding sinfulness, love's amazing greatness, and grace's fulness and freeness, as when first it saw and felt it in a sense of God's pardon. Oh, there is no human act which has such a tendency to melt, subdue, and win the whole being as that of forgiveness, be it judicial or parental, human or Divine. A heart that has become hardened in crime and steeped in sin, whom no reasoning could convince and no discipline could subdue, has at length been melted by mercy, conquered by forgiveness, and enchained by love. I quote an illustration of this truth. A soldier was brought before his commanding officer for a misdemeanor frequently committed and as frequently punished. He had been tried, flogged, and imprisoned; but, imperative and stern as military discipline is, all to no purpose. He was an old and incorrigible offender, whom no threats could dismay, and no infliction reform. As the officer was about to repeat his punishment, the sergeant stepped forward, and, apologizing for the liberty he took, said, "Sir, there is one thing which has never been done with him yet." "What is that?" enquired the officer. "He has never been forgiven." Surprised at the suggestion, and yet struck with its force, the officer meditated for a moment, then ordered the culprit before him. "What have you to say to the charge?" "Nothing, sir, only I am sorry for what I have done." "Well, we have decided to inflict no punishment on this occasion, but to try what forgiveness will do." The criminal, struck dumb with astonishment, burst into tears, and sobbed like a child. And what was the effect? From that moment he was another and a changed man. No longer the inveterate and hardened offender- a plague to his regiment and a dishonor to the service he became one of the most well-behaved and orderly men that ever wore the uniform or bore the standard of his sovereign. Forgiven, he became loyal and obedient: respect for military rule, and the fear of dishonoring the service and degrading himself, henceforth became to him a law and a shield. A similar incident in the life of Dr. Doddridge illustrates the same truth. Believing that there were extenuating circumstances in the case of a condemned criminal awaiting execution in Northampton Jail, Dr. Doddridge waited upon George III, and petitioned for his life. It was granted. Hastening back to his cell, he read the king's order of reprieve. The pardoned criminal rose, fell at his feet, and, clasping his person, exclaimed, "Oh, Sir! I am your servant, your slave for life! For you have purchased every drop of my blood." And shall a human forgiveness thus conquer, thus win, and thus inspire the fear of offending? O Lord, "there is forgiveness with You; for You have cast all my sins behind Your back, that I may serve You with reverence and godly fear all the days of my life, and henceforth to be Your servant, Your child forever!" Oh what a corrective of sin, what a motive to fear, what an incentive to obedience is God's forgiveness! "There is FORGIVENESS with You, that You may be FEARED." That which gives us the clearest, deepest, and most solemn view and conviction of God's holiness and love, inspires the most effectually a holy, filial, loving fear to offend Him. And where shall we find such an awful display of His holiness, and such overpowering demonstration of His love, as in the cross of Christ? Men do not fear God because they have no view of His holiness, no sense of His mercy, and no experience of His love. But God's forgiveness of sin furnishes the believer with the most convincing argument and with the most persuasive motive to live a pure, a holy, and a godly life. "The grace of God that brings salvation has appeared to all men, teaching us that, denying ungodliness and worldly lusts, we should live soberly, righteously, and godly, in this present world; looking for that blessed hope, and the glorious appearing of the great God and our Savior Jesus Christ."

Some suggestive reflections grow out of this subject.

Let no penitent soul despair of God's forgiveness "There is forgiveness with Him" for the vilest sinner, and pardon for the greatest sin. Listen to the divine exhortation and the promise: "Let the wicked forsake his way, and the unrighteous man his thoughts: and let him return unto the Lord, and He will have mercy upon him; and to our God, for He will abundantly pardon." See how reasonable and easy the conditions of the divine forgiveness! No, these conditions are privileges. What are they? To repent of your sins, to forsake your evil ways, to relinquish your rebellious 'thoughts' of God, your unbelieving 'thoughts' of Christ, your infidel 'thoughts' of Christianity, your skeptical 'thoughts' of the Bible, and to return to the Lord, and accept as the free gift of His grace His abundant pardon, and henceforth to do that which makes angels happy- love and serve Him! Do you not pronounce these conditions of the highest boon God can bestow or you receive, reasonable and righteous? Why then should you not be pardoned? Is there any difficulty but that which you yourself create? Is there any necessity why you should be lost, but that which your own persisted impenitence and unbelief render absolute? You allege that you cannot keep the law- Christ has kept it! That you cannot meet the claims of justice- Christ has answered them! That your sins are red like crimson, and countless as the stars- "the blood of Jesus Christ cleanses us from ALL sin." That you have no merit, and no worthiness with which to come before the Lord- "Ho, every one that thirsts, come to the waters, and he that has no money; come, buy, and eat; yes, come, buy wine and milk without money and without price." Then why will you die? How unnecessary, we repeat, that you should be lost! The violated law does not require it, incensed justice does not demand it, rejected mercy does not will it, and God, the great, the holy Lord God, has said, "As I live, says the Lord God, I have no pleasure in the death of the wicked; but that the wicked turn from his way and live; turn, turn from your evil ways; for why will you die?" PARDON, or PUNISHMENT? Choose! "WHO IS A GOD LIKE UNTO YOU, THAT PARDONS INIQUITY, TRANSGRESSION, AND SIN?"

Thus much for Divine forgiveness. But is there not a great practical precept based upon the doctrine of God's forgiveness of man, teaching and enforcing the duty and the privilege of man's forgiveness of his fellow-man? Most assuredly! "Be imitators of God as dear children" is the apostolic exhortation, and in no feature or act of God may we more closely resemble Him than in the full and frank forgiveness of injury and wrong, real or imaginary, inflicted by our fellows. There are few divine precepts around which there clusters so rich an accumulation of argument and exhortation, enforced by motives and appeals more solemn and pungent than that of human forgiveness- man's forgiveness of man. How pointed and impressive our Lord's own words: "If you forgive men their trespasses, your heavenly Father will also forgive you: but if you forgive not men their trespasses, neither will your Father forgive your trespasses." Who can read these words and not tremble at the thought of harboring in the heart an unforgiving spirit? And, then, touching the limit of human forgiveness, how emphatic the command of Christ: "Then came Peter to Him, and said, Lord, how often shall my brother sin against me, and I forgive him? until seven times? Jesus said unto him, I say not unto you, Until seven times: but, Until seventy times seven." And then follows the Savior's illustration of the royal forgiveness of the servant, in contrast with that same servant's unforgiving conduct towards his fellow-servant, concluding with these remarks: "So likewise shall my Heavenly Father do also unto you, if you from your hearts forgive not every one his brother their trespasses." We admit that, apart from divine grace, the last and hardest work of man is to forgive and forget a wrong, a wound, an injury inflicted by another; but, as it has been well observed, "He that cannot forgive others breaks the bridge over which he must pass himself; for every man has need to be forgiven."

Not less pointed is the teaching of the epistles on this precept of forgiveness. "Be kind one to another, tender-hearted, forgiving one another, even as God for Christ's sake has forgiven you. Be you therefore followers (imitators) of God, as dear children." Again, "Put on therefore, as the elect of God, holy and beloved, affections of mercies, kindness, humbleness of mind, meekness, long-suffering; forbearing one another, and forgiving one another, if any man have a quarrel against any: even as Christ forgave you, so also do you."

What need we more? Who can have felt the power and have tasted the sweetness of God's forgiving love, the "ten thousand talents" all forgiven, and then go his way and refuse to forgive the one hundred pence" owing him from his fellow-servant? It is in vain for you to expect, it is impudent for you to ask, of God forgiveness on your own behalf, if you refuse to exercise this forgiving temper with respect to others. There is an old English proverb by which even the Christian may be instructed, "Forgiveness and a smile are the best revenge." Forgiveness of an injury is the odor which flowers breathe when trampled upon; and a sweeter fragrance- more akin to the divine- nowhere exhales.

But the truest definition of forgiveness is the inspired one: "Overcome evil with good." And that this divine precept is designed as much to regulate our bearing towards unbelievers as believers is conclusive from the context: "Avenge not yourselves, but rather give place unto wrath.... Therefore if your enemy hunger, feed him; if he thirst, give him drink: for in so doing you shall heap coals of fire on his head." That there is a lamentable defect in the religion of many professors touching this divine precept of forgiveness of injury affords no slight evidence of the general unpractical character of the Christianity of the day. The deficiency of love among God's people, and of true hearty Christian union and co-operation in the Lord's work among members of different Christian communions, goes far to invalidate the claim which many assert to the discipleship of Christ. If a disciple of the loving, forgiving Savior, we have a right to enquire, "Where is your badge?" and if the response be, "What badge?" we reply in the words of the Lord Himself: "By this shall all men know that you are my disciples, if you have love one to another." With these words chiming on the ear, let us cease to cherish in our hearts an unforgiving, uncharitable, unforgetful spirit towards any who, intentionally or unwittingly, may have wronged and wounded us; confiding our character and vindication to Him of whom it is said, "Commit your way unto the Lord; trust also in Him; and He shall bring it to pass. And He shall bring forth your righteousness as the light, and your Judgment as the noonday." "Our Father who is in heaven; forgive us our trespasses as we forgive those who trespass against us." The grace of Christ and the prayer of faith will enable us to obtain this glorious and holy victory over ourselves.

WAITING AND WATCHING

"I wait for the Lord, my soul does wait, and in his word do I hope."
Psalm 130:5.

As the richest veins and the purest springs are found in the lowest strata of the earth, so in his profoundest soul-depths the believer often discovers the most precious truths, and is brought into the experience of the costliest blessings of the divine life. His deepest soul-excavations yield him the richest ore. We explore the treasures of God's word, and we unseal the springs of Christian experience, when, like David, we cry out of depths, or with Jonah, as from the 'fish's belly.' What thoughtful, spiritual mind can doubt this fact as it traces each verse of this remarkable psalm? A new vein of divine truth is opened, and a new spring of Christian experience is unsealed, in the passage we have now to consider faith's waiting and resting in soul depths. "I wait for the Lord, my soul does wait, and in His word do I hope." Mark the object, and then the ground, of David's waiting and resting posture. His sinking soul is as 'a weaned child,' and in that state has found a resting-place.

Mark, the OBJECT of David's waiting. "I wait for the Lord." Preparatory to this, David has learned two essential things in the depths- his sinfulness, and God's forgiveness. Having tasted the exceeding bitterness of the one, and the indescribable sweetness of the other, he is brought into a state of the most blissful repose; waiting for, and resting upon, his covenant God and Father. We know nothing of divine forgiveness until we are brought to the knowledge and confession of our personal sinfulness. Acquaintance with our own heart leads to an acquaintance with God's heart; a conviction that we are lost by sin, results in a conviction that we are saved by Christ. There are many religionists- religious in their own way- who are entire strangers to the wounding, and consequently are entire strangers to the healing: knowing nothing of the moral disease, they have experienced nothing of the spiritual remedy. It was not until the serpent-stung Israelite was conscious of the deadly virus flowing through his veins that he raised his eye, and rested it upon the brazen serpent uplifted in the wilderness, looking upon which he was healed. Nor is it until the Holy Spirit convinces of Satan's venomous sting, and of sin's fatal poison flowing throughout his whole being, that the soul-'ready to perish' looks in faith to Jesus, and is saved. But, we turn to this instructive verse. For whom does the Psalmist wait? "I wait for the Lord." How entirely is David divorced from the human, and how closely united to the Divine! We are so earthly that we gravitate to the earth- are "of the earth earthy;" we are so human that we cling to humanity, and make flesh our arm. And no little discipline is often required- the furnace seven times heated, and the knife of a two edge temper- before we are refined of the one and are pruned of the other. David had now found his true standing. He had fallen into great soul-straits, but, as we have shown, not below God. "The bright and Morning star" still shone resplendent above Him, and on it he fixed his believing eye. We cannot too frequently reiterate the truth, that it is impossible that a gracious soul can sink below God. There is that divine principle in him which utterly forbids it. When water ceases to seek its level, and light to flow back to the sun; when sparks fail to fly upwards, and the thirsty gazelle pants not for the water-brook, then may the living water in the soul cease to rise to the Source from where it came, and then may the divine love in the heart fail to flow back to the Heart from which it sprang.

But, again we ask, For whom did David wait? Higher he could not rise- lower would have plunged him in a yet profounder depth of soul dejection. Shall we put the question negatively? He did not wait for man. Long, wearisome and disappointing had been his waiting, had the creature been the object. "Cursed is the man that trusts in man, and that makes flesh his arm." How constantly we are drawing down upon us this dire curse! We build upon the creature, hang upon it, wait for it, until we wring the last drop from it as from a sponge, and nothing is left but emptiness and aridity. Oh, if but half the time we have spent in waiting on, and in waiting for, man-and at last finding him but a wounding reed and a broken cistern- had been spent in waiting upon and for the Lord, how much more successful and how much happier we should have been! But, sweet and holy the lesson taught us by David's example: "I wait for the Lord." Beyond this, as we have remarked, the soul cannot ascend; and to this Divine height every believer may rise. Nor is the flight of faith long or wearisome. The Lord is near to His people; "a very present help in time of trouble." David found it so: "You are near, O Lord." And so the Apostle: "The Lord is at hand." It is this consciousness of the Lord's nearness to us which disarms us of fear, strengthens us for service, and inspires us- howsoever deeply tried and assailed- with the boldness and strength of a lion! You have, perhaps, in a time of pressing need, of deep anxiety, or of earthly expectation, been waiting for weeks or months upon man. And still you wait, and hope deferred has made you sick at heart. Turn your eye from the creature to the Creator, from man to God, from false and powerless friends to your Heavenly, all-mighty, all-sufficient Father, and you shall not be ashamed of your trust. "My soul, wait you only upon God; for my expectation is from Him." "The Lord is my Portion, says my soul: therefore will I hope in Him." Is it sweet to lean upon one we love, hanging upon his arm for support, and reclining upon his bosom for sympathy? On whose wisdom we can unhesitatingly rely, in whose love we can confidently repose? Transfer this thought to God! How unutterable the blessedness, how vast the privilege, and how happy the result, of waiting upon Him who stands to us in the relation of our Father and Redeemer; our Brother and Friend; waiting the movement of His pillar of cloud; waiting the supply of His inexhaustible providence; waiting the comfort of His unchanging love; waiting for the fulfilment of the word of promise upon which He has caused our soul to hope! "My soul waits on the Lord." There does not exist a more privileged and holy condition of the soul than that of being entirely cast upon God. When the created arm fails to sustain, and the human heart to love, when earthly props give way, and affection and sympathy have fled their last asylum, when the barrel of meal is well near exhausted, and the cruse of oil distills its last drop-oh then to exclaim, "My soul, wait you only upon God; for my expectation is from Him" - this is a privilege indeed, a privilege eclipsing all others! If the Lord permits us a measure of creature support and sympathy- and this He sometimes does- it is in gracious condescension to the weakness of our faith and the craving of our constitutional temperament. Thus He dealt with the doubting Thomas. "Reach hither your finger, and behold my hands; and reach hither your hand, and thrust it into my side: and be not faithless, but believing." Sense was thus summoned to the aid of faith, and so helps it to believe. "Lord, help my unbelief." But the highest reach, and most God-glorifying act of faith is that expressed in David's words- "I wait for the Lord." Oh count it the richest experience of the divine life when, thus weaned and divorced from creature help, you are brought to wait only on the Lord, exclaiming,-"Now I have no prop, no supply, no sympathy, no comfort, but that which I find in Jehovah. I am shut up to Infinity alone: my help comes from the Lord." Passing from this rapid view of the Divine Object of David's waiting posture, let us look at the posture itself "I wait for the Lord, my soul does wait." We pronounce this a most blessed posture of the believer. It runs counter to everything that is natural, and, therefore, it is all the more a supernatural grace of the gracious soul.

In the first place, it is the posture of faith. It is a believing posture of the soul. The faith of the unbeliever- if faith it may be called- hangs upon air. He that builds below God builds upon shadows. Reposing his happiness and his hope upon his intellect, his health, his family, his life, he builds it upon the 'baseless fabric of a vision.' God never intended that the creature should find its happiness outside of Himself. "My people have committed two evils: they have forsaken Me, the Fountain of living waters, and have hewn out cisterns broken cisterns, that could hold no water." But here is the gracious soul hanging in faith upon God in Christ Jesus- upon the veracity of God to fulfil His promise upon the power of God to help him in difficulty- upon the wisdom of God to counsel him in perplexity-upon the love of God to shield him in danger upon the Omniscience of God to guide him with His eye-and upon the Omnipresence of God to cheer him with His presence, at all times and in all places, his Sun and his Shield. Oh have faith in God! The moment the soul can believingly repose upon Him, it ceases to be the sport of every wind and wave of circumstance and doubt, and drops its anchor on the firm and immovable bedrock of DIVINITY. It is also a prayerful posture. To wait for the Lord is not the languid waiting of indolence and indifference. This would be practical infidelity, the presumption of unbelief. The soul waiting for God is the soul waiting upon God. "They that wait upon the Lord shall renew their strength." The Lord often shuts us up to this waiting for His interposition on our behalf, that He might keep us waiting and watching at the foot of His cross- in earnest, believing, importunate prayer. Oh, it is the waiting for the Lord that keeps the soul waiting upon the Lord! We learn the sustaining, as well as the prevailing, power of prayer when brought into this holy posture in our soul-depths. Accept that as a most needful discipline that brings you into a prayerful waiting for the Lord. There is so much in daily life to stifle the spirit and hinder the exercise of prayer, so much that interposes itself between God and the soul; that the trial, the disappointment, the pressure, the "tarrying of the vision," becomes a powerful and precious help to the soul that is shut up to the taking hold upon God alone. "Be anxious for nothing; but in every thing by prayer and supplication with thanksgiving let your requests be made known unto God. And the peace of God, which passes all understanding, shall keep your hearts and minds through Christ Jesus." How instructive and precious are these words! There is first, the Prohibition- "Be anxious for nothing," anxious only to please God, and casting all other care upon Him. There is secondly, a Precept- "In every thing by prayer and supplication with thanksgiving let your requests be made known unto God." Give yourself to prayer, take hold on God, and with supplication blend the incense of grateful, prayerful thanksgiving. There is thirdly, the Promise- "And the peace of God, which passes all understanding, shall keep your hearts." How rich and how comforting! Walk in the prohibition, obey the precept, and God will fulfil the promise! All this is involved in David's soul-posture– I wait for the Lord, my soul does wait."It is also the posture of a patient waiting for the Lord. "I waited patiently for the Lord, and He heard my cry." There is not a more God-honoring grace of the Christian character than patience- a patient waiting on and for the Lord. Impatient of God's delays which we must ever remember are not God's denials- we cast about for means and ways of deliverance other than those in strict harmony with God's word and in simple confidence in His power. An impatient spirit kept Moses out of Canaan. An impatient act, an impatient word, what evil has it wrought!

But, to wait for the Lord and upon the Lord- His time of answer, His way of deliverance, His source of supply unburdens the mind of a thousand corroding anxieties, dislodges from the heart countless trembling fears, and preserves the feet from rushing into worldly, carnal expedients of relief, which would but plunge the soul into yet lower depths of difficulty and distress. Oh, cultivate this holy posture of a patient waiting for, and upon, the Lord! It is that Christian grace, the fruit of the Spirit, which will enable you to bear with dignity, calmness, and submission the afflictive dealings of your Heavenly Father, the rebuke of the world, and the wounding of the saints. In patience you will possess your soul, in patience you will suffer, and in patience you will do God's infinitely wise, holy, and approving will. It will strengthen you also in your work for the Lord. "By patient continuance in well-doing," you will "seek for glory, honor, and immortality, and eternal life." "Rest in the Lord, and wait patiently for Him." And whether buffeted for your wrong-doing, or for well-doing, you take it patiently, this is acceptable to God. Lord, endow us with this Christ-like grace of patience- patiently waiting the time and the way of Your interposition; patiently waiting you say to our soul, "I am Your salvation." "It is good that a man should both hope and quietly wait for the salvation of the Lord."

It is the posture of rest. A soul-waiting for the Lord, is a soul-resting in the Lord. Waiting and resting! Wearied with traversing in vain the wide circle of human refuges- coming to the end of all your own wisdom, strength, and resources your uneasy, jaded spirit is brought into this resting posture of waiting on, and waiting for, the Lord; and thus folds its drooping wings upon the very bosom of God. Oh how real and instant the rest found in Jesus! Way-worn and footsore, toilworn and garment-stained, battered with many a tempest and buffeted with many a wave, burdened, sinking, fainting, you have come to Jesus, and with the beloved disciple reclined your head upon His bosom; and, lo! in a moment the wind ceased, the billows slept, all was perfect peace and unruffled repose, and there was a great calm; and then, with the wondering mariners, you exclaim: "What kind of man is this, that even the winds and the sea obey Him!" Oh, there is no rest for the burdened, no peace for the anxious, no joy for the desponding, but faith in a divine, personal, and gracious Savior. Reposing in Him, however profound the depths of the soul, dark the clouds that drape it,

or surging the waters that overwhelm it, all is sunshine and serenity within. No external circumstances touch the under current of divine peace, which flows on in silvery sweetness, calm, unruffled, undisturbed. "When He gives quietness, who then can make trouble?" "The voice of the Lord is upon the waters," full of majesty, power, and tenderness, commanding, curbing, stilling them. "You will keep him in perfect peace whose mind is stayed on You, because he trusts in You." For what, beloved, are you waiting on the Lord? Are you waiting for the application of pardoning grace? No poor soul ever waited for God's absolution and waited in vain. If the Lord the Spirit has given you an insight of the evil of your nature, of the sinfulness of your heart, and a consequent contrition and sorrow, you are nearer to the joy of His salvation than ever Hagar was to the well of water flowing at her side. The Lord open your eye of faith to see it! O Lord, say unto my soul, I am your salvation! Are you waiting the answer to prayer? You shall not wait in vain. As soon will He cease to be God as cease to hear and answer the prayers of His saints. Prayer has an appointed time; though it tarry, wait for it. God's time is always the best and most opportune. He is never one moment too soon, nor one moment too late; never before, and never behind His time. "The vision is yet for an appointed time, but at the end it shall speak, and not lie: though it tarry, wait for it; because it will surely come, it will not tarry." Pray on, you seeking one; pray on, you child of sorrow; and if your petition is not immediately granted, learn that its tarrying is not its refusal, but meant only to test your sincerity, intensify your earnestness, invigorate your faith, and glorify your God.

Perhaps, in deep affliction and sorrow, you are waiting and watching for the "Consolation of Israel." Be it so. As sure as He came- though in infantile form- to the holy watchers in the temple, so sure will He come to you; and when, like the aged Simeon, you clasp Him in joy to your heart, with him you will be ready to exclaim, "Now, Lord, let You Your servant depart in peace!" Only wait until the crucible has melted, and the furnace has refined, and the rod has blossomed; only wait until affliction has accomplished its purpose, and sorrow has fulfilled its mission; and then Jesus, the "Consolation of Israel," will heal what He has made sore, and bind up what He has wounded, pouring into your desolate, bleeding heart the oil and the wine of His sympathy and love. We reach the ground of the Psalmist's waiting upon the Lord: "And in His word do I hope." Here is the only sure basis of faith and hope of the gracious soul, sinking in its profound and fathomless depths. God's word is the only plank to which faith clings, and clinging to which, will float the tempest-tossed, wave-buffeted soul safe to the shore. It is in God's word, and not man's, the believing soul hopes. Forever His word is settled in Heaven! Heaven and earth shall pass away, but not one word of God shall fail. God's word is truth. "All the promises of God are yes and Amen in Christ Jesus." The believing, sinking soul trusts in nothing human, in nothing visionary, when it trusts in the revealed word of God. All other foundations are but as the shifting, treacherous sand. All expectation is visionary and delusive but that which draws its inspiration from, and rears the structure of its hope upon, the eternal, unchangeable word of the living God. God's revealed word is a divine, immortal rock, building upon and hoping in which, the soul shall before long spring from its lowest depth to its loftiest height, chanting its "new song before the throne of God and the Lamb."

Oh! whatever else fails you, cling to God's word. Part with all yes, with life itself- rather than part with it. "Cast not away your confidence which has great recompense of reward."

"This Book, this holy Book, on every line
Marked with the seal of high Divinity;
On every leaf bedewed with drops of love
Divine, and with the eternal heraldry
And signature of God Almighty stamped
From first to last; this ray of sacred light,
This lamp from off the everlasting throne,
Mercy took down, and in the night of Time
Stood, casting on the dark her gracious bow;
And evermore beseeching men with tears
And earnest sighs to read, believe, and live."

Watching for the Morning

"My soul waits for the Lord more than those who watch for the morning: I say, more than those who watch for the Morning." -Psalm 30:6.

Having dilated upon the waiting posture of the Psalmist's soul, we now approach the consideration of its profound intensity. "My soul waits for the Lord more than those who watch for the morning: I say, more than those who watch for the morning." The image is exquisitely poetical, as it is singularly expressive. The natural morning is, perhaps, the most beautiful, and to many the most welcome, part of the day. To the languid and weary invalid it is especially and indescribably so. The night, it may be, has been long and dreary; sleep has fled the pillow, pain has tortured the limb, and the whole network of nerves quivers with indescribable suffering. But yet more distressing than this: the mind, in close sympathy with the body, still more acute has been the mental restlessness and disquietude of the night watches. It is an acknowledged phenomenon that, every material object and spiritual conception assumes a more distorted form and a darker hue at night than at any other season. The circumstances of life, the events of providence, the discipline of God, all borrow from its gloom and solitude their shape and complexion.

The physical and the mental thus in the closest and most painful sympathy, oh, how the invalid, weary and exhausted, longs for the morning! How welcome the first trembling streak of light- the first soft blush of day! And when the night-lamp (the moon) expires, and the morning dawns bright and cheering, how exquisitely lovely and welcome its advent! The air laden with a thousand odors, the flowers sparkling as with countless diamonds, all nature robed in virgin beauty, and vocal with the lark's morning hymn of praise, the whole scene presents a picture which the imagination may conceive, but which the pencil and the pen fail to portray. For the advent of this scene the sick one, weary and faint, longs and watches. "Those who watch for the morning."

Passing from this sketch of the natural morning, we are prepared to contemplate the spiritual morning of the soul. There are various spiritual mornings in the history of the Church of God, collectively and individually, on which it may be profitable briefly to meditate. The First Advent of our Divine Lord was the most significant and momentous morning of all that succeeded. What a fact in the history of the world when the "Bright and Morning Star" first appeared, heralding the rising of the "Sun of Righteousness." Up to that moment the moral world was wrapped in the profoundest Egyptian darkness. And yet, at no former or even later period of its history had philosophy, science, and art attained to so pre-eminent a standard of perfection.

Let the history of Greece and of Rome testify. Sensible of the profound degradation of the people, the appalling ignorance and vice into which the most classic and civilized nations were plunged, men arose fired with the intense desire to dispel the one and to reform the other. They speculated, philosophized, and moralized. Science developed its mysteries, are unveiled its splendors, philosophy discoursed, eloquence thundered, and poetry sang, but all to no effect. The multitude remained sunk in stolid ignorance, pagan superstition, and degrading sin. "The world by wisdom knew not God." It was at this crisis, when the wisest of the world's philosophers- Socrates and Plato for example- acknowledged that, as the state of the people then was, there was no human means of reforming them; sighing for a revelation, they expressed a hope, and even an expectation, that God would at some future time make such a discovery of Himself, and such a revelation of His will, as would dispel the cloud of darkness in which they were involved.

It was at this juncture, when the night of the world was the darkest, lo! the Sun of Righteousness arose with healing in His wings! Oh, what a glorious morning was this! Then was the magnificent prediction concerning Him fulfilled- "And He shall be as the light of the morning, when the sun rises, even a morning without clouds." "And there were in the same country shepherds WATCHING FOR THE MORNING abiding in the field, keeping watch over their flocks by night. And, lo, the angel of the Lord came upon them, and the glory of the Lord shone round about them: and they were very afraid. And the angel said unto them, Fear not: for, behold, I bring you good tidings of great joy, which shall be to all people. For unto you is born this day in the city of David a Savior, which is Christ the Lord." Then was heard the angels' advent anthem which broke in the sweetest music over the plains of Bethlehem- "Glory to God in the highest, and on earth peace, good will to men."

Let us in faith often go to Bethlehem, and muse upon that wonderful thing that has come to pass- "The Ancient of days" becoming an infant of days! "God manifest in the flesh." May this advent-morning of joy dawn upon us! May this "day-spring from on high" visit our souls, translating us from darkness into light, from the children of the night into the children of the day!

And what is the new creation in conversion but the dawn of morning to the soul? The greatest change in individual character, the most momentous event in its history, is, the advent of the day of grace in the soul. The creation of myriads of worlds is nothing in comparison. God created the universe out of nothing; but in conversion God has to uncreate before He creates the soul anew- to pull down before He builds up, to kill before He makes alive. Until this auspicious era dawns, until this day of grace breaks, all is spiritual darkness; the night of sin, of ignorance, and of enmity against God supremely reigns. The eyes of the understanding are closed, the veil is on the heart, and the whole soul is wrapped in a pall of more than Egyptian darkness. But, the new creation's morning comes. He who at creation's dawn said, "Let there be light" -and light was, -in the new creation speaks the word, "Let there be light," -and light is. Jesus Christ, the Sun of Righteousness, rises upon the soul, scatters the clouds of spiritual ignorance, sin, and unbelief; and, lo! the day dawns, and the brightest morning that ever broke upon the soul fills it with the joy and radiance of a new creation. "If any man be in Christ Jesus, he is a new creature (new creation)· old things are passed away; behold, all things are become new." With the solemn, startling fact confronting us- "Except a man be BORN AGAIN, he cannot see the kingdom of God," how essential and momentous does this morning of grace in the soul appear!

And when to this positive condition we contrast the negative that, baptism is not conversion; and that, the Lord's Supper is not conversion; and that, a reformation of life is not conversion; that, an intellectual acquaintance with the truth is not conversion; that, works of beneficence and deeds of charity are not conversion- that, with all this the night of spiritual darkness may still envelop the soul, unbroken and unillumined by a solitary ray of spiritual, quickening, saving light with what overpowering solemnity do the Savior's words fall upon the ear- "Marvel not that I said unto you, YOU MUST BE BORN AGAIN." "It is the Spirit that quickens; the flesh profits nothing." "So is every one that is born of the Spirit."

But, oh- we repeat- how bright and blessed this day-dawn of grace! If the sunrise in creation is a scene of surpassing loveliness, its beauty and splendor pale before the glory of the new creation in the soul. Its advent may be faint and gradual. For the most part- except in seasons of especial outpouring of the Spirit, when, as it were, a nation is born in a day- conversion begins from the most incipient stage, and by slow and almost imperceptible degrees advances to maturity.

The analogy of nature suggests this idea. It is said that, the darkest period of night is that which borders the closest on the break of day. May not this phenomenon furnish an illustration of our thought? How often does conversion transpire at a time when the subject appears the farthest from the day of grace, and yet, perhaps, in reality the nearest! The cup of iniquity is brimmed and running over; the unhappy servant of sin has reached the end of the tether; Satan, the Pharaoh of this world, has demanded of his oppressed and down-trodden slave, the full toll of bricks without the straw- in other words, some task of heinous iniquity, for the performance of which both the physical and mental powers are in capacitated. Sin has exhausted its powers of invention; iniquity has reached its height of guilt; the world can offer no new attractions of folly; infidelity has achieved its boldest stroke; and the unhappy victim, abandoning all hope of amendment, has made 'a covenant with death, and with hell is at agreement.'

It is then that Jesus of Nazareth passes by. It is then the darkest hour of the moral night that the first ray of the Divine Sun breaks upon the soul. Some startling providence, or some impressive sermon, some personal appeal, or some spirit-stirring volume- perhaps a page of God's own word-has roused the soul from its deep sleep of death, and starting from its unconsciousness and its dreams, wakes to behold the dawn of a new day, a new life, a new creation, a new world! O blissful moment when Jesus thus enters the soul, scattering all the clouds of ignorance and sin, of atheism and unbelief, of self-righteousness and worldly folly; and, creating for Himself a new orbit, henceforth fills and floods its entire being with the life and radiance of his grace, glory, and love.

At creation's dawn the "morning stars sang together for joy;" but sweeter far the music of angels when the 'new creation,' emerging from its chaos of darkness and death, floats into being, instinct with life, glowing with beauty, and melodious with song- God's holiest, greatest, and most sublime work!

"That was a time of wondrous love,
When Christ my Lord was passing by;
He felt His tender pity move,
And brought His great salvation near.
"Guilty, and self-condemned, I stood,
Nor thought His mercy was so near;

When He my stubborn heart subdued,
And planted all His graces there.
"My eyes were sealed, the shades of night
Over all my mental powers were drawn;
He spoke the word, 'Let there be light!'
And straight the day began to dawn."

Perhaps, my reader, you are anxiously watching for this bright morning of grace? The night of your soul has been long and dreary. Sick of sin, of self, and of the world, you sigh, and long and look for the dawn of a new existence, a higher life, another world in which you may no longer live for self, but for God; no more for time, but for eternity. Oh welcome this longing, this watching, this looking, as heralding the daybreak of grace to your soul! The first light of morning is very soft, the first blush of day very faint. So, ofttimes, is it with the day-spring from on high in the soul. And yet, faint and trembling as is the first ray of spiritual light, it yet is as really, as essentially day, as when shining in its noontide splendor.

The most imperfect consciousness of sin, the first serious thought- a sigh, a tear, a desire, an upward glance of the eye- are harbingers of the dawn of that "shining light" in the regenerate soul "which shines more and more unto the perfect day." Wait on, watch on, you Christ-longing, Christ-seeking soul! for you shall not watch and wait in vain. The Savior's promise is- "Ask, and it shall be given you; seek, and you shall find; knock, and it shall be opened unto you."

Every weeping Christ-seeker shall be a rejoicing Christ-finder; for, 'the Lord has not said to the seeking seed of Jacob, Seek my face in vain.' Pray on, and watch on, until Jesus manifests Himself to your soul, and the Sun of Righteousness has risen upon you with healing in His wings.

And then, there is a more advanced stage of the Christian life the watching for the morning in the night-season of afflictive dispensation. Every child of God has his night of sorrow and of tears. The mournful experience of the Psalmist is often reproduced in that of many of the Lord's people. "I am weary with my groaning; all the night make I my bed to swim; I water my couch with my tears." "My sore ran in the night, and ceased not: my soul refused to be comforted." "With my soul have I desired You in the night." "I meditate on You in the night watches."

Who among all God's saints are exempt from this long, dreary night of weeping? The Lord of saints Himself was not. His whole life- from the moment of His birth in the stable, to the hour of His death upon the cross- was one unbroken night of weeping.

"From Bethlehem's Inn to Calvary's Cross,
Affliction marked His road,
And many a weary step He took
To bring us back to God."

"Born of a woman, and made under the law," our Divine Lord, the moment His infant feet pressed our earth, came under the curse, began His work of obedience, and wove the first thread of that seamless, stainless Robe of Righteousness for the full and free justification of His believing people; which, when completed, He dyed in the purple stream of His own heart's blood upon the cross. "He was a man of sorrows, and acquainted with grief."

Beloved, you are, perhaps, now in a measure assimilated to your suffering Lord. It is with you a night of grief and solitude, of weeping and watching. God has smitten you. The hand of the Almighty is upon you. What is the cup your Father has given you to drink? Have riches fled? has health faded? have friends changed? has death bereaved? Are earthly hopes blighted? worldly expectations disappointed? human schemes frustrated? Is your path shaded? your life lonely? your actions misunderstood? your motives misconstrued? your work unrewarded? your sensibilities wounded? your spirit crushed? Be it so. Jesus passed through all this before you, and you are but treading the lonely, tearful path He trod; and now, like Him, you are "one that watches for the morning."

Oh how you long for the first ray of light, for the first dawn of day- the morning of joy that will assuredly succeed your night of weeping! Nor shall you watch in vain! Such is the divine promise in which you are permitted and invited to hope. "Weeping may endure for a night, but joy comes in the morning." That was a long, dark night of weeping with the dear disciples tossed upon the broken waters of the lake. "It was the fourth watch of the night, and Jesus had not come." But, just when the tempest was the strongest, and the billows were the highest, and the night was the darkest, lo! the form of Jesus was seen in the grey twilight, walking upon the surging billows, and approaching the tempest-tossed vessel; and they cried out for fear, mistaking Him for a ghostly spirit. And then was heard His own familiar and loved voice rising above the tempest,"Be not afraid; it is I," and then in a moment dawned upon them the "morning of joy," and they fell in transport and adoration at His feet.

Thus, beloved, will it be with you. You are whole nights in your watchtower looking for some ray of hope, some means of deliverance, some source of supply, some drop of comfort, some avenue of escape from a present and a crushing trial. You shall not watch in vain. It is recorded of Wellington when on the field of Waterloo, as the battle waged hard, and affairs assumed a critical and threatening aspect, he was heard to exclaim, "Would it were night, or that Blucher had come!" Reversing the time, you, in the heat of the conflict with suffering and trial, with temptations and tears, often exclaim, "Would that it were morning, and that my Savior had appeared!" And so it will be! The Lord will not leave you comfortless. It shall not be all night, all sorrow, all tears. Wait on the Lord, and wait for the Lord, 'as one that watches for the morning.' Joy will succeed your sorrow, laughter your tears, and your long and dreary night will dissolve into the splendor of perfect and endless day. "Men see not the bright light which is in the clouds: but the wind passes, and cleanses them."

Then there is the morning that precedes the night of spiritual and mental darkness. How many a child of the day is walking as in the night; and how truly is he "as they that watches for the morning." Painful as this soul-depth is, the discipline is needful to its growth and maturity. How imperfectly, if at all, should we sympathize with Christ in His soul-desertion on the cross, were we entirely exempt from this discipline of soul-darkness, through which all the children of the light and of the day are called, more or less, to pass.

Tempted in all points like as we, yet without sin, we must touch the Savior at all points of His life. There must, to a degree, be assimilation, coincidence, conformity of the Body with the Head. As in the darkest night the stars glow with softer effulgence, so in the gloomiest days of adversity, temptation, and sorrow, the saints of God- the stars of His right hand- shine all the more- chastened and resplendent in those graces of faith, patience, and love, which, perhaps, are never reflected in such perfection, or are seen to such advantage as when his sky is draped with its darkest hues.

Child of the day, walking in darkness, anxiously watching for the light, be of good cheer! The morning dawns, the day breaks, there is a bright light in your cloud, and soon the darkness will have passed, and you shall ever more walk in the light of God's countenance, the joy of Christ's person, and the comfort of the Holy Spirit.

"Give to the winds your fears;
Hope, and be undismayed;
God hears your sighs, and counts your tears;
God shall lift up your head.
"Through waves, and clouds, and storms
He gently clears your way;
Wait His time- your darkest night
Shall end in brightest day."

But, the believer, from the lowest depths of his experience, waits and watches for a brighter morning, more glorious and enduring far than yet has broken upon this dark and sinful world. The night-season of death is, to the believer in Jesus, the day-dawn of life: the lowest degree of grace, the germ and the pledge of the highest degree of glory. Death is not really death to him who has life in Christ; it is but the shadow- the substance Jesus met and overcame when He died upon the cross. "Who has abolished death, and has brought life and immortality to light by the gospel." And yet, how the faithful shrink, awed by the thought of death, and appalled by the act of dying!

It was a beautiful experience of the pious sister of Gregory of Nazianzus, when dying. Faintly pronouncing the words of David, "I will lay me down in peace," she fell asleep, safe in the arms of Jesus. What wonders at that moment burst upon her sainted sense! First, and beyond all, the sight of her glorified Lord. The welcome of sister spirits, the melody of rejoicing saints, the anthems of holy angels, the bright seraphic host, the purer, more perfect, and transcendent splendor of the exalted Trinity. The last taint of impurity effaced, the last groan of suffering hushed, the last sigh of sorrow stilled, the last tear of grief wept, the last fear of death quelled. Freed from ignorance and error, anxiety and folly, carnality and worldliness, not a cloud now shades, or a wavelet ruffles, the brightness and serenity of her glorified spirit.

No longer looking forward to death as a sturdy and relentless foe, she looks back upon it as the Israelites upon the pursuing Egyptians, lifeless upon the shore; and thus rises and swells her song of victory- "Sing you to the Lord, for He has triumphed gloriously; the horse and his rider has He thrown into the sea." Lord, let me die a death as calmly! my last end as peacefully and hopefully as hers! But, it is not with the night of death- a soft sleep though it be- but with the sun-rise of life, the day-dawn of glory, that we have to deal.

"And is this Heaven? and am I there?" will be the first exclamation of wonder and ecstasy bursting from every new inhabitant the moment it enters! For this morning of glory the believing soul ardently, hopefully watches. How many are nearing its coasts! how many have reached its border! how many are passing it now! Sick and suffering saint of God, don't you long to be there? Are you not ready to say to every object and being that would detain you on these plains of sin and pain and sorrow, in the words of the Divine Angel to the wrestling patriarch, "Let me go, for the day breaks"?

"Only waiting til the shadows
Are a little longer grown;
Only waiting until the glimmer
Of the day's last beam is flown;
Until the night of earth is faded
From the heart, once full of day;
Until the stars of heaven are breaking
Through the twilight, soft and gray.

"Only waiting til the reapers
Have the last sheaf gathered home;
For the summer-time is faded,
And the autumn winds have come.
Quickly, reapers! gather quickly
The last ripe hours of my heart;
For the bloom of life is withered,
And I hasten to depart.

"Only waiting til the angels
Open wide the mystic gate,
At whose feet I long have lingered,
Weary, poor, and desolate.
Even now I hear their footsteps
And their voices far away;
If they call me, I am waiting
Only waiting to obey.

"Only waiting til the shadows
Are a little longer grown;
Only waiting until the glimmer
Of the day's last beam is flown;
Then, from out the gathering darkness,
Holy, deathless stars shall rise,
By whose light my soul shall gladly
Tread its pathway to the skies!"

But, we wait the morning of the Resurrection! The saints of God are called the "children of the resurrection." "If by any means they might attain unto the resurrection of the dead" in Christ, and share with them the splendor and the bliss of that bright morning, they willingly relinquish the worldling's portion- his honors, pursuits, and pleasures to "have part in the First Resurrection, upon whom the second death shall have no power." Do not the generality of the saints deal too imperfectly with the two great Resurrections- the Resurrection of Christ, as sealing and confirming the completeness of His atoning work; and the Resurrection of His saints, as 'having their perfect consummation and bliss, both in body and soul, in Christ's eternal and everlasting glory'?

And yet, what truths more divine, what facts more certain, what hopes more precious, than these? Realizing "the power of Christ's Resurrection" in your soul, you will die to sin and live to righteousness, daily ascending more and more into a higher region of the Christian life. Oh, marvelous the life-quickening into deeper holiness that flows from faith's daily apprehension of "the power of Christ's Resurrection!" It must be so. If the believer is dead with Christ, he is also risen with Christ; and if risen with Christ, he possesses the most potent and precious motive to set his mind, not on things on the earth, but "above, where Christ sits on the right hand of God."

Scarcely less influential is the contemplation of his own Resurrection to eternal life, when the trumpet of the Archangel shall sound, and the dead in Christ shall rise first. For this 'morning of joy,' succeeding our 'night of weeping,' let us be as "they that watch for the morning," Standing whole nights in our watch-tower, longing for the first dawn of that bright and blissful day.

The Coming of the Lord- the brightest and most glorious morning of all- supplies a last and magnificent illustration of our present subject. Truly, we have, in our reflections, 'kept the best wine until now.' The Second Coming of Christ is the pivot upon which all the future glory and blessedness of the saints turn. "If in this life only we have hope in Christ, we are of all men most miserable." But the personal and "glorious appearing of the great God our Savior" unveils to faith's eye that "blessed hope," for which we wait and long and watch- even the coming of "the Savior, the Lord Jesus Christ: who shall change our vile body, that it may be fashioned like unto His glorious body, according to the working whereby He is able even to subdue all things unto Himself."

Nor shall the Bride wait long the coming of the Bridegroom. "The night is far spent, the day is at hand." All things and all events in the Church and the world point to His near approach. Am I reminded that certain great epochs of time are to transpire, and events in history are to take place, before the blessed hope is realized? Conceded! But, is it necessary that long centuries must roll round before that time and those events arrive? What says the Scriptures touching the events that will precede and herald the coming of the Lord? "He will finish the work, and cut it short in righteousness: because a short work will the Lord make upon the earth."

Are you calculating the time for the accomplishment of these events- the 'bud and foliage of the fig-tree' -by your own line of measurement? "Beloved, be not ignorant of this one thing, that one day is with the Lord as a thousand years, and a thousand years as one day." Oh, yes He will 'cut short the work in righteousness.' "A nation shall be born in a day." In one night the 'fig-tree' will burst into bud and blossom, and fill the world with its fragrance and its fruit. The Jews will return the remnant according to the election of grace will be converted. The Euphrates will be dried- the time of the Gentiles will come; Antichrist will rise and fall- and then shall appear the Son of Man in the clouds of heaven, and with Him all His saints. "For if we believe that Jesus died and rose again, even so them also who sleep in Jesus will God bring with Him."

Then will burst upon the long dreary night of this groaning, travailing creation, the light and splendor and music of the Resurrection morn! "The dead in Christ shall rise first: then we who are alive and remain shall be caught up together with them in the clouds, to meet the Lord in the air: and so shall we ever be with the Lord. Wherefore comfort one another with these words."

The soul and body, now once more and forever re-united, shall enter glory, and become an inhabitant of that land of which it is said, "And there shall be no night there:" no night of ignorance, no night of suffering, no night of sorrow, and best and brightest of all-no night of SIN, but one perfectly holy and endless day! "Watchman, what of the night? Watchman, what of the night? The watchman said, The MORNING comes." You bright and glorious morning! speed your advent! Dawn upon this dark and sinful world! The saints wait and sigh, pray and watch for Your appearing. "COME, LORD JESUS, COME QUICKLY!"

"Oh, glorious will that gathering be,
From every clime, of every race,
When hearts long lonely then shall see
Him, and each other, face to face!"

Hoping in the Lord

"Let Israel hope in the Lord: for with the Lord there is mercy, and with Him is plenteous redemption." -Psalm 130:7.

To what a sacred 'height' does the soul of the Psalmist now rise! Mounting as with eagle wing, he soars above all cloud and storm, and stands, with the Apocalyptic angel, in the very center of the sun; springing from the lowest "depths," and planting his foot on the topmost height of faith's ladder, he summons the whole Israel of God to imitate his ascent and participate his joy. "Let Israel hope in the Lord: for with the Lord there is mercy, and with Him is plenteous redemption."

Such is the privilege, and such may be the experience of all the saints. They, who in their soul-depths are found prayerfully and believingly waiting on the Lord; shall assuredly be found "hoping in the Lord." Prayer strengthens faith, and faith begets hope, and hope, lifting the soul superior to all circumstances of trial and despondency, folds its golden pinions upon the very bosom of God. "Those who wait upon the Lord shall renew their strength; they shall mount up with wings as eagles; they shall run, and not be weary; and they shall walk, and not faint." "I wait for the Lord, my soul does wait, and in His word do I hope." "Let Israel hope in the Lord." These words suggest three interesting and instructive points of reflection the object, the character, and the encouragement of the Christian's hope. May the Holy Spirit guide and bless our meditation thereon!

We have upon the threshold of our subject a sharply defined line of essential difference between the believer and the unbeliever, the converted and the unconverted, the Church and the world, touching the object of hope. The unconverted are described by the inspired penman as "having no hope," Appalling description! Interpreting it but in its relation to the present world, can the imagination, in its boldest flight, picture a condition more pitiable and appalling than that of entire hopelessness? Divest man of hope, and you have plunged him in the darkest, deepest abyss of despair.

Take from the sufferer the hope of relief, from the sick the hope of life, from the exile the hope of return, from the captive the hope of release, from the condemned the hope of reprieve, and you have quenched the last spark of life, have dashed from the lips the last drop of comfort, shading the entire scenery of existence with the heaviest clouds of despair and woe. It is hope-the first true offspring of reason, the recognition of purer intelligence- that rocks the cradle of suffering infancy, paints its golden tinge upon the dismal cell of the prisoner, lulls to balmy repose the couch of languor, sits proudly upon the warrior's crest, and visits alike, faithfully and kindly, the poor man's hut as the rich man's palace.

"What is hope? The beauteous sun,
Which colors all it shines upon!
The beacon of life's dreary sea,
The star of immortality!
Fountain of feeling, young and warm,

A day-beam bursting through the storm!
A tune of melody, whose birth
Is, oh, too sweet, too pure for earth!
A blossom of that radiant tree
Whose fruit the angels only see!
A beauty and a charm, whose power
Is seen, enjoyed, confessed each hour!
A picture of that world to come,
When earth and ocean meet
The last overwhelming doom!"

But what is all human hope, as to its nature and object, but a phantom and a dream as the foam on the crest of the billow, the shadow on the mountain's brow- unsubstantial and fleeting? Yet, how does the soul cling to it! How do men, looking only to the things that are seen and temporal, cling to human hopes, pursuing a bubble, building upon a shadow, grasping the wind! How unreal, unsatisfying, and evanescent the hope that rests in the creature, that is built on the world, that clings to wealth and honor and life! All for a while looks true and bright- hope investing the present and painting the future with its most gorgeous and attractive hues. But, adversity comes, and reverse comes, and sickness comes, and death comes, and eternity comes, and then the sky is darkened, and the flowers droop, and the music is hushed, and all human hopes one by one grow dim and expire as the day fades into evening, and the evening deepens into night. Oh the folly of building the hope of happiness below God, out of Christ, and this side of Heaven! Chase no longer the phantom, the dream, the shadow of human hope, of earth-born good; but, acquaint your self with God, seek Christ, and fix your thoughts, your affections, your whole being, upon the world of stern and solemn reality towards which time is rapidly speeding you. "This is life eternal, that they might know You the only true God, and Jesus Christ, whom You have sent."

We now turn to the Christian's hope- the only true, substantial, and living hope of the soul. How truly and impressively the passage under consideration defines this hope. "Let Israel hope in the Lord" -not in the creature, not in himself, not in his own righteousness- but, "let him HOPE IN THE LORD."

There is everything in God to inspire and encourage hope. Oh, it is a marvelous truth- a truth, had it not been divinely revealed, the mind could not have discovered, nor the heart have believed it that, the soul of man, lost in sin, might again hope in God! But examine the foundation of this hope, and all wonder ceases. Christ is the Foundation, the Object, and the End of the believing sinner's hope. "The Lord Jesus Christ, who is our hope." There is but one divinely revealed and assured hope of heaven, and it centers wholly and exclusively in the Savior of sinners. The Atonement of Christ touches the soul, and meets its case at every point. There could be no hope of the sinner's pardon and justification consistently with Divine Justice, Holiness, and Truth apart from the obedience, death, and resurrection of the Lord Jesus Christ.

The remission of the sin and the justification of the sinner, in the exercise of mere Mercy, would have subverted the authority of the Divine Law, and have prostrated the honor and dignity of the Divine Government. It follows then, as strictly logical as it is soundly scriptural, that a hope of eternal happiness, reposing upon the abstract attribute of Mercy, must prove fallacious and fatal, since, based, upon the principle of one Divine perfection, exhibited and exercised at the expense, compromise, and destruction of all the others; this necessarily involving the undeifying of the Being and the overthrow of the moral Government of God.

In pardoning the sin, and in justifying the sinner, the penalty incurred and the obedience demanded must be met. The law must be honored, justice satisfied, holiness secured, and the righteousness, dignity, and glory of the moral Government of God displayed and magnified in the eyes of the whole universe. Let an ingenuous and thoughtful mind pause and enquire how could God exhibit His infinite abhorrence of sin, and vindicate the holiness of the law; how exact the stern penalty incurred by the one, and meet the unbending requirements of the other- by saving the sinner on the sole basis of Mercy alone? Impossible!

But, behold the plan! The Son of God, by His sinless obedience, has met all the precepts of the Law, magnifying and making it honorable, -the Law Giver thus becoming the Law Fulfiller, and by His sacrificial death has answered all the demands of justice, satisfying its every claim, and paying every farthing of the debt; and now the glory of God appears infinitely greater in the salvation of one sinner than it could have appeared in the eternal destruction of every being of the human race!

Oh what imagination can fully conceive, or language adequately describe, the glory which accrues to God from the Atonement and Sacrifice of the Lord Jesus Christ, who is our hope! Countless worlds, plunged eternally into hell, could never have so exhibited God's holiness and justice and truth, or have presented such a perfect display of His glory before angels, men, and devils, as the sacrifice of His beloved Son upon the cross of Calvary. "I have glorified You on the earth: I have finished the work which You gave me to do."

Behold your true and only hope of heaven! You are, perhaps, bowed to the earth under the sight and conviction of your sinfulness; you have come to the end of all your own doings, perfection, and merit; you are on the brink of despair! Look up! there is hope now! "Christ died for the ungodly." "This Man receives sinners." "He who comes to me I will in no wise cast out." "Christ is the end of the Law for righteousness to every one that believes." "And when they had nothing to pay He frankly forgave them both." "The blood of Jesus Christ His Son cleanses us from all sin." "By grace are you saved."

With such a cluster of gospel and precious announcements, extending to the most sinful and necessitous, who need despair? who will not hope? Innumerable as your sins are, aggravated as is your guilt, bankrupt of all merit and fitness and claim but that which your character and case as the chief of sinners supplies you yet may hope in Christ. "Let Israel hope in the Lord," though Israel's name be "of sinners the chief." The only room found for despair beneath the cross is in the case of him who approaches with an unhumbled spirit, an unbroken heart, pleading some worthiness of his own, and with a price in his hand dreaming that salvation may be purchased with the base coin of human merit, religious doings, and creature worthiness.

But no! the character is portrayed, the terms are prescribed, upon the ground of which the 'great salvation' provided by the Father, finished by the Son, and applied by the Spirit, becomes our present, gratuitous, and inalienable possession. "The whole need not a physician; but they that are sick. I came not to call the righteous, but sinners to repentance." "Him that comes to me I will in no wise cast out." Hope, then, in Christ Jesus! Hope in His love to receive you; hope in His blood to cleanse you; hope in His righteousness to justify you; hope in His free and boundless grace to accept and save you "just as you are." "Let me not be ashamed of my hope." "Let Israel hope in the Lord."

God is revealed as "the God of hope." An expressive and precious title this! It infinitely surpasses the picture of hope as thus exquisitely painted by a noble poet:

"The rainbow to the storms of life,
The evening beam that smiles the clouds away,
And tints the morrow with prophetic ray."

But what is the most exquisite conception of hope compared with the hope thus portrayed by an inspired pen: "The God of hope fill you with all joy and peace in believing, that you may abound in hope, through the power of the Holy Spirit"? On the groundwork of the Atonement of the Son of God, the Father becomes "the God of hope" to all who abjure every other hope, and hope only in Him.

There is no circumstance in which we may be placed, no condition in which we may be involved, no lack or danger or impossibility draping our path with dark and lowering clouds of dark despair, but the soul may yet fix its hope in God. How sweet and assuring is the hope of a child in a parent's love, care, and protection! Such a Father is ours! We may hope in His forgiveness, to cancel our greatest sins; in His wisdom, to guide our most intricate perplexity; in His power, to raise up from the lowest depth; in His love, to soothe our profoundest grief; in His resources, to supply our every need; and in His faithfulness, to make good the word of promise upon which He has caused our souls to hope.

Our folly, yes, our sin, is in building our hope in something other than God. No marvel that our creature cistern- the loveliest should break, mocking and intensifying the thirst it promised to slake. No marvel that our staff- the strongest- should break beneath us, piercing the hand that leant upon it too trustfully and too fondly. Oh, what is the lesson God is daily teaching us, which yet we are so reluctant to learn, but this the folly and the sin of confiding too implicitly in the shadow of creature good, earthly possessions, and human hopes; still more, in self-wisdom, power, and government?

But, let your condition be ever so extreme- human friendship disappointing you, earthly supplies failing you, human sympathy refused you, and dark despair enthroned grimly and coldly upon your heart- there yet is hope in God! The Lord has withered this fleshly arm, and dried up that creature spring, and blown upon this worldly hope, that you might be shut up to Him alone. Never was He so near as at this moment, when human help is far; never so loving, and compassionate, as now, when human love has failed!

"The Lord is at hand. Be anxious for nothing; but in every thing by prayer and supplication with thanksgiving, let your requests be made known unto God." "For with the Lord there is mercy." What an encouragement have we here to hope in God! There is mercy- infinite mercy, pardoning mercy, justifying mercy, sanctifying mercy, helping mercy- in Him in whom you hope. The Lord "delights in mercy;" and because there is mercy with Him, the child of God, though often brought very low in circumstances and position, may yet hope for succor, comfort, and deliverance. You may not find mercy in the creature, still less in your own self; for, self-reflection, self-reproach, and self-abhorrence, in the remembrance of your sins and backslidings, may place you beyond the region of hope; but, because in Him there is mercy- infinitely precious, overflowing mercy you may 'hope against hope' that God in Christ will never leave you, nor forsake you.

Thus, the encouragement you have to hope in God, when all other hope has expired, springs from that mercy in His nature which has been truly described as His 'darling attribute;' for, "He delights in mercy." "Behold, the eye of the Lord is upon those who fear Him, upon those who hope in His mercy." "Let Your mercy, O Lord, be upon us, according as we hope in You. "

"And with Him is plenteous redemption:" another and a yet more assured ground of hope in the Lord. Redemption is the one and sole foundation of the sinner's hope of heaven. Every ray of hope expired, until re-kindled by Christ, who by His obedience and death "opened the kingdom of heaven to all believers." Amid the agonies of Jesus and the convulsions of nature, hope sat smiling upon the cross; and from out the thunder of the Law and the lightning of justice- the earth quaking, the rocks rending, the sun darkening her sweetest, softest music was heard- "It is finished!" More resplendent still will be her arch, and sweeter still her voice, when, amid the "wreck of matter and the crush of worlds," the "ransomed of the Lord shall return, and come to Zion with songs and everlasting joy upon their heads;" and the "New Jerusalem" will be seen "coming down from God out of heaven, prepared as a bride adorned for her husband." Then will the believer's hope of glory- often obscured, often doubted, yet never entirely relinquished- blaze forth in its unclouded, full-orbed splendor, crowned with glory, honor, and immortality.

"Eternal Hope! when yonder spheres sublime
Pealed their first notes to sound the march of Time,
Your joyous youth began-but not to fade,
When all the sister planets have decayed;
When, wrapped in fire, the realms of ether glow,
And heaven's last thunder shakes the world below,
You, undismayed, shall over the ruins smile,
And light your torch at Nature's funeral-pile."

The believer is "saved by hope." Not that hope is the cause of salvation, but the means of its enjoyment; not salvation, but its end. The regenerate soul is a divine orb of hope circling around its great Center- "the Lord Jesus Christ, who is our hope" -from which it springs, whose glory it reflects, and whose praise it chaunts. A hope of glory which thus has Christ for its foundation, Heaven as its end, must be a "good hope through grace," the possession of which will never make ashamed, but which, like a fine setting sun, will grow larger and brighter, until lost in the fullness and splendor of eternal fruition.

It is "plenteous redemption." All that emanates from God must necessarily be a reflection of Himself. Flowing from the infinity of His nature, it must partake, in some degree, of the plenitude of His Being. Now, no work of God confirms this fact and illustrates this truth as His master work of man's Redemption. In it God unsealed all the resources of His Divinity. By no other means could He have accomplished it. Every atom- so to speak- of Divinity, every perfection of His nature, was employed in working out the plan of human salvation. Had one attribute stood aloof, had one perfection been wanting, the entire scheme would have fallen to the ground. The creation and destruction of myriads of worlds would not, and could not, have supplied such an evidence of His Being, or have made such a display of His glory, as the Redemption of the Church by the sacrifice of His Son. Upon this glorious truth is predicated the blessed announcement that, "with Him is plenteous redemption."

Behold the ground of your hope! Have you been taught by the Holy Spirit your sinfulness and sin? Have you had such an insight into the plague of your heart as to bring you well-near to the verge of despair? Does your guilt appear so heinous as to place you beyond the pale of God's Church and the reach of His salvation? Listen to the declaration- "Let Israel hope in the Lord: for ... with Him is plenteous redemption." Disbelieve it not- reject it not for a moment. When the number of your sins and the turpitude of your guilt exceed the virtue of the blood, and out-distance the grace of Christ, and exhaust the plenitude of God's redemption, then, and not until then, may you abandon yourself to the iron grasp of despair.

Oh, yes! there is with God "plenteous redemption." What case can it not meet? What sin can it not cancel? What sinner can it not save? "Where sin has abounded, grace does much more abound." Where sin has prostrated, grace much more uplifts; where sin has destroyed, grace much more repairs; where sin is victorious, grace is triumphant; where sin has usurped the throne, much more does "grace reign through righteousness unto eternal life."

Sin-burdened soul, there is plenteous redemption for you! "Bread enough in your Father's house, and to spare." "The blood of Jesus Christ His Son cleanses us from ALL sin." Could the plenteousness of His redemption be affirmed in words more touching, or in terms more assuring? "Let the wicked forsake his way, and the unrighteous man his thoughts: and let him return unto the Lord, and He will have mercy upon him; and to our God, for He will ABUNDANTLY PARDON." "You, Lord, are good, and ready to FORGIVE; and PLENTEOUS in mercy unto all those who call upon You." See, then, that, in the stupendous matter of your salvation you do not limit that which in its efficacy Christ has made illimitable; that you append no conditions to that which God has made unconditional; that you attempt not to purchase by fancied worthiness of your own that which the infinite merit of Jesus has made unpurchasable and most free.

A few practical deductions will close this chapter. It follows from the preceding exposition that it is of the utmost importance, of vital moment, that we make sure of the nature and foundation of our hope. There are false hopes of heaven, as there are false hopes of earth. It was a most holy prayer of the Psalmist, which every believer should, in a daily examination of his real state before God, breathe- "Let me not be ashamed of my hope." Oh, what multitudes are cherishing a spurious hope of heaven! building their hope, not upon the Rock Christ Jesus, but upon the quicksand of their own righteousness! Look well, my reader, to the nature and foundation of your hope for the future! In settling the question of its reality, assume nothing as true which has not God's word for its ground and its proof.

It is written: "Except a man be born again, he cannot see the kingdom of God." It is written: "If any man be in Christ Jesus, he is a new creature." It is written: "Without holiness no man shall see the Lord." It is written: "He that believes not shall be damned." Heaven and earth shall pass away, with all their greatness and grandeur, but God's word shall never pass away! Look, then, well to your hope after death. See that it is built upon Christ alone- a Divine Redeemer, a Personal Christ, a sin-atoning Savior-Christ, the Alpha and Omega, the First and the Last, yes, the all and in all of your hope of glory. May the language of the Christian poet embody and express the true foundation of your hope of heaven:

"My hope is built on nothing less
Than Jesus' blood and righteousness;
I dare not trust the sweetest frame,
But wholly lean on Jesus' name.
On Christ, the solid Rock, I stand:
All other ground is sinking sand.
"When darkness seems to hide His face,
I rest on His unchanging grace;
In every high and stormy gale
My anchor holds within the veil.
On Christ, the solid Rock, I stand:
All other ground is sinking sand.
"His oath, the covenant and blood,
Support me in the whelming flood;
When all around my soul gives way,
He then is all my hope and stay.
On CHRIST, the solid ROCK, I stand:
All other ground is sinking sand."

An equally natural, and scarcely less important, deduction from the subject of this chapter, is the necessity of guarding prayerfully and vigilantly against every subtle influence tending to impair the vigor and shade the luster of our hope of heaven. We can but present in a summary form some of the more prevalent and potent influences contributing to this mournful result. The world- its friendships and pursuits, its recreation and religion- is a powerful and ever sleepless foe. Against it we must be on our guard, would we have the lamp of hope burn brightly in the soul. Sin, superficially viewed and lightly committed, unrepented of and unforsaken, will weaken the strongest and shade the brightest hope of the soul. The neglect of public and private means of grace living at a distance from the fountain of atoning blood- the feet daily unwashed, and the conscience unpurified- tampering with error, and listening to false doctrine- the perusal of a light, fictitious, worldly literature- the novels of the day- will certainly and seriously compromise the stability, enjoyment, and brightness of this precious grace of the Spirit.

Oh, guard with sacred jealousy and sleepless watchfulness this holy, heavenly light "the God of hope" has kindled within your soul, more vigilantly than the vestal virgin, her lamp; or the priest, the temple light of God's house. "Every man that has this hope in Him (Christ) purifies himself, even as He is pure." And "in hope of eternal life, which God, that cannot lie, promised before the world began," see that you "present your body a living sacrifice, holy, acceptable unto God, which is your reasonable service." The God of hope grant that, by the avoidance of these evils, and the cultivation of these means, your hope of heaven, like the sun kissing the horizon, may grow larger and more brilliant, until it sets in the glory and splendor of perfect and endless day! Then, "your sun shall no more go down; neither shall your moon withdraw itself, for the LORD shall be your everlasting light, and the days of your mourning shall be ended."

"The hope that is laid up for you in heaven" -how comforting, sustaining, and sanctifying! Your path to its full realization will, in many of its stages, be thorny and shaded, trying and lonely. If there is a royal road to heaven, it is that traveled by the King Himself, impurpled with His blood, vocal with His groans, and hallowed with His strong crying and tears. Along this road we are traveling. And how blessed and assured the hope! It is the hope of dwelling forever in our Father's home! Over its threshold sickness shall no more pass, spreading its mantle of suffering, languor, and decay! Bereavement shall never enter- with its shadow, bitterness, and separation! Sin shall not intrude- tainting, wounding, beclouding! Affliction, trial, and pain shall be utterly and forever unknown, no more wringing the heart with anguish, and mantling the soul with woe. Perfectly holy, the soul will be supremely happy, forever with kindred spirits, "AND FOREVER WITH THE LORD."

Let nothing move you from this hope. Let not prosperity or adversity, the creature or the world, induce you for a moment to relinquish your hold- shaded and feeble though your hope of heaven, through Jesus, may be. It may be but a ray- the faintest scintillation- nevertheless, "hold fast the profession of our faith without wavering." "Cast not away therefore your confidence, which has great recompense of reward."

Has the last sickness come? Is death approaching- heart and flesh failing, Jordan's waves murmuring at your feet? Oh, cling only and firmly to Christ! Look not so much to your hope as to Him who is your hope! The realization may be feeble and fluctuating, the prospect of heaven misty and dim; nevertheless, "Jesus Christ is the same yesterday, today, and forever." Your hope may wane, its pendulum may oscillate as between earth and heaven, but its Object and its End are as fixed, immovable, and stable as the throne of the Eternal. "Which hope we have as an anchor of the soul, both sure and steadfast, and which enters into that within the veil; where the Forerunner is for us entered, even Jesus."

How soothing to the sad hour of bereavement is the hope of a certain reunion and individual recognition of the loved ones who have a little while preceded us to glory! If in heaven we are not to know and not to love those whom on earth we knew and loved, with whom we took sweet counsel and traveled many a weary stage of our journey, then one essential element of heaven's happiness would be lacking, which even earth, with all its sin and sorrow, affords. "I must confess," says the holy Baxter, "as the experience of my soul, that the expectation of loving my friend in heaven powerfully kindles my love to them while on earth. If I thought I should never know, and consequently never love them after this life, I should remember them with temporal things, and love them as such; but I now delightfully commune with my pious friends, in a firm persuasion that I shall commune with them forever; and I take comfort in those that are dead or absent, believing that I shall shortly meet them in heaven, and love them with a heavenly love." They are there waiting and looking for our coming!

Fight on, toil on, hope on, you soldier of Christ, you laborer for Jesus, you tried and suffering one! Soon you shall put off your travel-stained garments, unclasp your dust-covered sandals, lay down your pilgrim-staff; and, attired in glory-robes, enter the palace, and feast your eyes upon the beauty of the King forever. "The golden palace of my God,

Towering above the clouds, I see;
Beyond the cherubs' bright abode,
Higher than angels' thoughts can be!
How can I in those courts appear
Without a wedding garment on?
Conduct me, You Life-Giver, there;
Conduct me to Your glorious throne!
And clothe me with Your robes of light,
And lead me through sin's darkest night."

Final and Full Redemption

"And He shall redeem Israel from all his iniquities." -Psalm 130:8.

What a graceful and appropriate conclusion of this comprehensive and instructive Psalm! Like the sun, it dawns veiled in cloud, it sets bathed in splendor; it opens with soul-depth, it closes with soul-height. Redemption from all iniquity! It baffles the most descriptive language, and distances the highest measurement. The most vivid imagination faints in conceiving it, the most glowing image fails in portraying it, and faith droops her wing in the bold attempt to scale its summit. "He shall redeem Israel from all his iniquities." The verse is a word-painting of man restored, and of Paradise regained- a condition infinitely transcending the holiness and beauty of their original and pristine creation. Iniquity is more than forgiven- it is utterly effaced and eternally forgotten. The soul is more than saved- it is justified, adopted, and glorified.

Thus, by the wonderful redemption wrought by Christ, we gain infinitely more than we lose. Man, clad in the righteousness of God, shines with a luster- and Paradise, closed against all "that defiles, and works abomination, or makes a lie," blooms with a beauty never possessed before sin tainted the one, or the curse blighted the other. Redemption, final and full, is the theme of our present chapter. "He shall redeem Israel from all his iniquities."

In unfolding this subject, our starting point must be the central truth- Israel's Divine Redeemer. The Person of Christ is the center of Christianity. Remove this, and the whole system is destroyed. He is the Foundation; destroy this, and the entire fabric falls. All the doctrines and precepts, all the promises and hopes of the gospel and of the believer, converge towards Him as their common center, and revolve around Him as their life giving Sun.

There never was a period in Eternity in which the Redeemer of men did not occupy His original and essential place as God. The Second Person of the Trinity, His throne has ever been the central one of Heaven; and His present original and essential glory as God, constituted Him the central Sun of all beings and of all worlds, upholding the universe by His arm, ruling it by His will, and shaping its history by His providence. But, passing by the central position and power of the Redeemer in the empire of Creation and Providence, let us concentrate our thoughts upon the yet more appropriate and essential illustration of this thought- His central position in the kingdom of grace. Here we behold Him in His proper place, and in His full orbed glory. It will be instructive to trace His appointment as the Redeemer of His Church to the hands of the Father.

Our Lord's was not a self appointed office. Most voluntary as its assumption was, He assumed not one line of action independent of the Father. This, indeed, could not possibly have been; since, essentially one in nature, they were essentially and indivisibly one in purpose and mind, in will and heart. It would have been as impossible that the Father could have acted independently of the Son, or the Son to have acted independently of the Father, as for one mind to conceive two opposite purposes, or one will two contrary volitions. Hence our Lord affirmed, "I and my Father are ONE." "My Father works hitherto, and I work." "Verily, verily, I say unto you, The Son can do nothing of Himself, but what He sees the Father do: for what things soever He does, these also does the Son likewise." "I can of mine own self do nothing: as I hear, I judge: and my judgement is just; because I seek not mine own will but the will of the Father which has sent me." "He that has seen me, has seen the Father."

What a glorious view does this unfold of the equality of the love of the Father and of the Son in the redemption of Israel from all iniquity! The plan of Redemption was the united conception and scheme of the Godhead, and originated in the Divine love of the ever-blessed Three in One. "God so loved the world, that He gave His only begotten Son." The misapprehension of many- and a more unscriptural and dishonoring one could not exist is, that the Redemption of Christ was the inspiration and origin of the love of the Father! In other words, that the Atonement was the cause, and not the effect, of God's love; that, Christ died to purchase and procure the love of the Father; and not- which is the only scriptural and logical view of the subject- that, the death of Christ was the consequence, and not the cause- the effect, and not the origin of God's love. In view of this stupendous mystery of love and grace, may we not pause, and exclaim, "Thanks be unto God for His unspeakable Gift"?

Oh, it is a sweet reflection, that, when I lay my head upon the bosom of Jesus, I feel the throbbings of my Father's heart; that, when I bend my ear to the words of Jesus, I listen to the sound of my Father's voice, of which my Savior's is the gentle and gracious echo. "He that has seen me, has seen the Father." Let the truth encourage you, that in confiding your soul in faith to the hands of Christ you are assured of God's acceptance, since in dying upon the cross, and in receiving sinners, He acts in perfect harmony and concert with the purpose and mind, the will and heart of God.

The personal fitness of the Redeemer for the redemption of Israel is so palpable, and rests on so scriptural a basis, as to admit of not a moment's argument or doubt. It consisted essentially of the union of the two natures of Christ- the Divine and the Human. This union of the Infinite and the finite was indispensable. They could not have accomplished the work alone and apart from each other. The Divine was essential to the efficacy of Christ's death, the Human equally as essential to the death itself. As essential Divinity could not die, neither could mere Humanity atone. Hence, "the great mystery of godliness, God manifest in the flesh." Herein lies the Redeemer's main fitness for the office thus divinely invested and thus voluntarily assumed. His Human nature- as free from the taint of sin as His Divine enabled Him to give a perfect obedience to law and a full satisfaction to justice. His Divine nature- absolutely and essentially Divine stamped His righteousness with such divine perfection, and His blood with such sovereign efficacy, as enabled Him to redeem, now and forever, the Israel of God from all iniquity. A not less essential element of fitness in Israel's Redeemer was the love- the great, the unparalleled love- which constrained Him to embark in the work of our Redemption.

Were I asked to mention the most prominent perfection in the marvellous scheme of our salvation, I would unhesitatingly cite that of Divine love. It was not that the law was honored, and that justice was satisfied, and that the debt was paid, that invested our Redemption with a glory so resplendent; it was the great love of God in devising, and the equal love of Christ in executing, and the divine love of the Spirit in applying, the wondrous expedient of our salvation. LOVE outsteps every other perfection, love eclipses every other attribute; love is the most gorgeous and resplendent tint in the "Bow round about the throne," -the Bow of the covenant-salvation uniting and blending in their sweetest and most beauteous harmony, all the perfections of God, -the perfection of DIVINE LOVE the most conspicuous and resplendent of all.

"Christ also has loved us, and has given Himself for us an offering and a sacrifice to God for a sweet-smelling savor." Fall prostrate before this stupendous, this marvellous, this unheard of love, and yield to it the supreme faith and homage of your entire being. Doubt not its reality, limit not its vastness, question not its freeness; but, believe it, accept it, live it- and you shall be saved.

From this rapid view of Israel's Redeemer let us briefly advert to Israel's Redemption. Redemption! it is the most significant and precious word in God's vocabulary. We shall, if saved, be spelling out that word, and yet never fully grasp its meaning, through all eternity. Studying, yet never entirely learning its meaning; extracting, yet never exhausting its sweetness; gazing upon its effulgence, yet never wholly absorbing its glory; chanting its song, yet never ending its praise!

And what is this Redemption? Our passage leaves us in no doubt. It is a "redemption from all iniquity." No other redemption could have met our case; redemption from mere affliction and sorrow, from sickness and suffering, from anxiety and care, would still have left us the degraded servant of sin and the willing slave of Satan, bound and fettered by the chain of the most galling bondage, and delivered over to the most appalling woe. But, Christ's redemption is from the cause of all affliction, suffering, and death- it is our "redemption from all iniquity." "He shall redeem Israel from all iniquity." Let us briefly look at this stupendous truth in two or three of its more essential points.

It is a redemption from the curse of sin. The entire removal of the curse by Christ is a point very much underrated and overlooked by the believer. The Divine blessing, in its fullest sense- His redemptive blessing- could not be upon us did one atom of the curse still remain unrepealed. But, our Divine and gracious Redeemer hurled the entire incubus from His Church when, 'born of a woman and made under the law,' He was "made a curse for us." Marvellous truth! The Son of God accursed for man's sin, looked upon and dealt with as the accursed one; cast out of Jerusalem as too accursed to die within its holy precincts! "Jesus also, that He might sanctify the people with His own blood, suffered outside the gate." What then is the blessed deduction from this truth? That, the cup of the divine curse being thus exhausted by our Divine Redeemer- not a drop lingering upon the brim- there remains nothing but the Divine blessing. The curse of the law is removed from the person and works, from the afflictions and sufferings, of the believer; and, henceforth, nothing but the Divinest BLESSING rests upon all that he is, and upon all that he does, and upon all that he endures; whatever the cross he bears, the suffering he endures, or the cup he drinks.

"Your blessing is upon Your people." His blessing is upon your person, for it is "accepted in the Beloved;" upon your labors, for they are "not in vain in the Lord;" upon your trials, afflictions, and sorrows, "For our light affliction, which is but for a moment, works for us a far more exceeding and eternal weight of glory." Oh, what a soul-height is this, out of our depths of darkness and woe!

Christ's work is also a redemption from the guilt of sin. Sin's guilt is a fearful incubus, bowing the soul to the dust. No temporal calamity can be compared with it, no physical suffering equal it. It shades every scene of beauty, embitters every cup of joy, disturbs the harmony of every song of gladness, is "the worm that never dies" of the lost in hell. But, the Redemption of Christ exempts us from this canker-worm, releases us from this crushing weight. His righteousness repealed the curse of the law, His Atonement cancels the guilt of sin. If the sacrifices of the law sanctified to the purifying of the flesh, "how much more shall the blood of Christ, who through the Eternal Spirit offered Himself with out spot to God, purge your conscience from dead works to serve the living God?"

Thus, it is the blood of Christ that purifies the conscience, effacing its guilt; and healing its wound. And when a fresh sense of guilt is contracted- as fresh acts of sin assuredly will; the secret of daily purification and walking in communion with God will be found in an immediate renewed application to the blood of the Atonement, the conscience afresh sprinkled from every trace and vestige of sin's guilt. We cannot press this habit of constant washing too earnestly upon the reader. The tense in which the apostle places the blood before us teaches and enforces this habit: "The blood of Jesus Christ His Son CLEANSES us from all sin." It is in the present tense. Our blessed Lord, whose blood was on the eve of being shed, refers to this continuous application of the blood in that memorable conversation with Peter. Recognizing his past cleansing- "he that is washed'-Jesus strenuously insists upon a present one, the laving of the feet, of which His own condescending act at that moment was so impressively symbolic and significant. This may have suggested the apostle's exhortation, long after he had learned it from Jesus- "to whom COMING, as unto a living stone" -now coming, always coming to Jesus, as the Rock of our salvation, as the strength and support of our daily life. Oh, upon what a holy soul-height this continuous living upon Christ will keep us, raised above the world, above trials, above temptation, above self, preserving the mirror of the conscience unclouded, and unsullied by a breath!

The subduing of the power of sin in the believer, is not less a result of Christ's Redemption. To pardon the commission and to cancel the guilt of sin, and yet leave its reign undisputed and its scepter unbroken, would but neutralize all the happier effects of Christ's atoning work. Sin is a powerful tyrant. Long after its overthrow it still exists in the regenerate a dethroned, uncrowned despot; its sting extracted and its venom destroyed, but still retaining sufficient power to wound and distress the soul. Despoiled of its empire, like the Canaanites of old, It is yet domiciled in the land, making perpetual invasions and assaults on the camp of Israel; demanding on their part sleepless vigilance and perpetual conflict. Thus, the work of sin-mortification and world-crucifixion must go on, that, by a gradual process of defeat and extermination, the spiritual Canaanites, like the typical ones of old, are driven out "little by little," until the last enemy is destroyed, and the victorious paean of triumph floats sweetly from the lip of the conqueror-

"Thanks be to God, who gives us the victory through our Lord Jesus Christ."

Now, for this gradual subduing of indwelling sin, the Redemption of Christ graciously and effectually provides. The promise that, "sin shall not have dominion over us," that, it shall never again recover its throne and sway, as before- its scepter over the soul broken; it rests upon the provision Redemption has made for this blessed result. That Redemption involves all supplies of grace from Christ, the indwelling of the Holy Spirit, the sanctifying influence of the truth, the power of prayer, and the hallowed results of God's afflictive dispensations. All these appliances God employs to promote our sanctification, and to make us holy, as He is holy.

A blessed height of the soul is that when the believer can look down upon his old sins and habits, lying mortally wounded at his feet, dying daily to their power and reign. Oh, there is no real happiness this side of heaven apart from personal holiness! God Himself could not be perfectly happy were He not perfectly holy. And just in proportion as we approximate to His supreme holiness, we approximate to His supreme happiness. How thankful should we be, amid all our depths of adversity, tribulation, and sorrow, that there are sacred heights on the earth where we may walk with God in sweet fellowship, in divine assimilation, and in filial love, -our souls arrayed in "the beauty of holiness."

My soul! let your one and supreme aim be, a loftier standard of personal holiness, a more exalted soul-height of unreserved consecration to God- the ear, the hand, the foot, as of old, sanctified with atoning blood, thus consecrating your members to the Lord: the ear, attentively listening to the voice of His word; the hand, diligently employed in His service; the foot, swift to run the race that is set before us- "looking unto Jesus." Thus, "the grace of God .... teaching us that, denying ungodliness and worldly lusts, we should live soberly, righteously, and godly, in this present world," will have in us its perfect work, lacking nothing. Lord, what is lacking in my grace, supply; what is weak in my faith, strengthen; what is low in my Christian life, raise; what is languid and ready to die, quicken and revive, that I may stand complete in all the will of God.

It only remains that we include in this catalogue of redemptive blessings, the believer's exemption from sin's condemnation. Sin has a condemning power. "He that believes not is condemned already." But our blessed Lord Jesus Christ was condemned for sin, and condemned sin, on the cross. The sins of His elect were arraigned, tried, condemned, and executed, when He cried, "It is finished." Hence the glorious declaration with which the Apostle opens that remarkably rich and magnificent chapter in his epistle to the Romans: "There is therefore now no condemnation to those who are in Christ Jesus." The salvation of Christ redeems Israel from all legal condemnation. The world may condemn, the saints may condemn, conscience may condemn, but God never! "He that believes on Him is not condemned. " Well may we exclaim, in the adoring language of the Apostle, "Thanks be unto God for His unspeakable gift!"

But the saints' full and final Redemption is yet to come. The passage evidently bears this prospective interpretation: "He shall redeem Israel from all iniquity." We have seen in the course of this chapter, that, while salvation involves a release from the guilt, despotism, and condemnation of sin, it does not provide an amnesty in the present perpetual conflict with its indwelling existence and power. Sin will remain in the regenerate to the last of life. But a full redemption awaits the believer. It is most true, that, the moment the Christian is released from the body, he is in a state of perfect holiness as it regards the soul; but the full redemption of the body is yet to come. The Apostle, in the epistle to the Romans just quoted, thus puts it: "And not only they, but ourselves also, which have the FIRST FRUITS of the Spirit, even we ourselves groan within ourselves, waiting for the adoption, to wit, the redemption of our body." The time is coming when we shall no longer be chained to a corrupt body, a living corpse, tainted with sin, mortified with corruption, assailed by disease, suffering, and death. A glorious resurrection awaits us- a full redemption from the power of the grave. "O death, I will be your plagues; O grave, I will be your destruction!"

But, before we enlarge more fully upon this redemption of the body from corruption, it may be wise to signalize the great and august event, although already alluded to, in connection with which it will transpire. This perfect redemption of the believer awaits the Second Coming of the Lord. "For the Lord Himself shall descend from heaven with a shout, with the voice of the archangel, and with the trump of God: and the dead in Christ shall rise first: then we who are alive and remain shall be caught up together with them in the clouds, to meet the Lord in the air: and so shall we ever be with the Lord." It is towards this blessed hope that faith turns its longing eye. Looking beyond our partial emancipation at death, it fixes its earnest and unfaltering gaze upon a coming Redeemer.

We know that death- terrific as the spectacle is to some- is a merciful deliverance of the believer from all the ills of the soul; for, absent from the body, the soul is instantly present with the Lord. This emancipation, however, is but partial. The body- as much redeemed by Christ's precious blood as the soul, is still locked in the rigid embrace of death, and is still the corrupt prisoner of the grave, pending the Advent of Him who is the "Resurrection and the Life." But, when this glorious Epiphany arrives- when the Son of Man shall appear in the clouds of heaven, encircled by all "the spirits of just men made perfect" -then, the full redemption will transpire: and the soul, now re-united to the body, will ascend into a higher region of glory and blessedness, even the Third Heaven, where Jehovah dwells, waiting the arrival of the New Heaven and the New Earth, down upon which the whole Church will descend, "prepared as a bride adorned for her husband."

We must keep distinctly in mind the connection of the coming of the Lord and the resurrection of the saints. These two events perfectly synchronize. They are inseparable. "Our citizenship is in heaven, from where we look for the Savior, the Lord Jesus Christ, who shall change our vile body (the body of our humiliation) that it may be fashioned like unto His glorious body." And here the pen falters in its attempt to describe the beauty, the glory of that risen body. It will be "a spiritual body," that is, a body free from the taint and grossness of the flesh, and yet material; with the same organs of sense, the same active limbs, capable of the same physical and intelligent communion with its fellows as now, yet free from all that now mars and interrupts that communion. No physical deformity will mar its symmetry; no existence of sin will taint its purity; no ravages of disease will torture its limbs; and no assault of death will imperil its existence. Oh, what an epoch that will be in the history of the redeemed, when from the hill, the valley, and the sea- from the venerable churchyard and the picturesque cemetery, -the 'dead in Christ' shall come forth, all resplendent with the glory, and hymning the new song of the resurrection morn! Let us comfort one another with this prospect!

One practical thought before we close this chapter. Be it our earnest desire to 'attain unto this resurrection of the holy dead' by an increasing knowledge of Christ and 'the power of His resurrection.' And if we are thus risen with Christ mystically, let us rise with Christ spiritually, by setting our affections more earnestly upon the things that are above, where Christ sits at the right hand of God. Then, 'when Christ, who is our life, shall appear, we also shall appear with Him in glory- and so be forever with the Lord!

Soul Heights

"The Lord is my strength, and He will make my feet like hinds' feet, and He will make me to walk upon my high places." -Habakkuk 3:19.

"O my dove, that art in the clefts of the rock, in the secret places of the stairs, show me your face, let me hear your voice; for your voice is sweet and your face is lovely." Song of Solomon 2:14

These words, though not taken from our Psalm, are yet in such close harmony with its teaching, and suggest so befitting and graceful a close of its exposition, that we venture to append them, as sustaining and crowning the leading truths of this volume. They speak of HEIGHTS- of "high places" belonging to the believer, upon which God makes His saints to walk as with the hind's swift and sure foot. "He will make my feet like hinds' feet, and He will make me to walk upon my high places."

The only true elevation of man is that of the soul, and the only individual who really knows anything of soul elevation is he whose standing before God is in Christ Jesus. "In Your righteousness shall they be exalted." It is not always in the 'depths' with the Christian. He who is invariably so, reflects but imperfectly the true nature, and brings great dishonor upon the divine character, of Christ's holy gospel. Our blessed Lord describes His people as "lights to the world." But with many of His disciples, alas! how dimly does their light burn! Were the world to take its notion of the religion of Jesus from their illustration of its character and spirit, what injustice would be done both to that religion and its Divine Author!

The true element of the gospel is holy joy. It is emphatically the "joyful sound." "Behold, I bring you good tidings of great joy, which shall be to all people. For unto you is born this day in the city of David a Savior, who is Christ the Lord." It possesses the elements of all joy. It reveals Jesus, the Savior of the lost; it proclaims a Salvation for the chief of sinners, full, finished, free; it leads to a Fountain open for cleansing the uncleanness of all sin; it unfolds a righteousness without a seam, a stain, or a flaw, for the full and free justification of the ungodly; it supplies the most powerful motive to all holiness; while it unseals the deepest, sweetest springs of all consolation and comfort to the broken heart and the wounded spirit. Surely, there are no soul-depths here, except the depths of divine love, the depths of holy joy, the depths of strong consolation!

But, what are some of these "high places" of the Church of God upon which He makes His people to walk? "He will make me to walk upon my high places."

Need we place in the foreground, the high place of Conversion, upon which all that are saved are made to walk? It is the first and leading step to each ascent of the believer. In what a low place does the soul of man walk until it reaches the 'high place' of converting grace! The highest life of an unregenerate man is, in a spiritual sense, but a low life; it is in the 'depths' of sin and selfishness, of enmity against God, and of ruin against his own being. Take the most intellectual pursuit, the most refined enjoyment- be it science, or art, or music- viewed as bounded only by the present life, as ending in self, having no relation to the higher interests of the soul, the claims of eternity, and the glory of God- how low the life! In the strong language of inspiration, "He feeds on ashes" - "feeds on wind."

Is this life worthy of a rational, responsible, immortal being? Is it worthy of one soon to confront death, judgement, and eternity? soon to appear at Christ's bar, to give an account of a stewardship of intellect, and of rank, and of wealth, and of time, and of influence, the most responsible and solemn ever entrusted to mortal hands? Is this the life you are living, my reader? is this the mere existence in which you vegetate? Rise to a higher life, a nobler purpose, a more glorious end! Don't you know that, "we must all appear before the judgement seat of Christ, to give account of the deeds done in the body"? That "every one must give account of himself to God"?

But conversion reverses this sad picture. When the soul is 'born again,' it emerges from its lower life, and ascends into a new, a divine, a heavenly life- a life from God, and for God; a life in Christ, and by Christ, and with Christ; a life best described by the language of one who lived it fully, lived it nobly, lived it until crowned with a martyr's diadem- "For Me to Live Is Christ."

Oh, upon what a 'high place' does the soul born from above now walk! Truly, it is a new birth, a re-creation! Old things have passed away, and God's Spirit has made all things in that life new. How revolutionized the whole soul! It has awakened as from a dream, a trance, a death, and finds itself in a new world of thought and feeling, of life, holiness, and love. It never really lived until now. Oh the blessedness of now truly living, and of living for God! The feeling of his soul finds its truest exponent in language of the apostle: "None of us lives to himself, and no man dies to himself. For whether we live, we live unto the Lord; and whether we die, we die unto the Lord: whether we live, therefore, or die, we are the Lord's."

God makes His people's feet like hinds' feet, to walk in the high places of His love. Who can describe the sacredness and preciousness of this walk? "God is love," and to enjoy God's love, and to dwell in God's love, is to walk upon the highest place on earth, and in the closest proximity to heaven. The love of God shed abroad in the heart by the Holy Spirit, is to dwell in God and God in us. How elevating this walk! How it lifts us above the dark clouds of trial and sorrow that float beneath, into a high and luminous atmosphere, in which we can read, in the light of His love, all our Heavenly Father's dealings with us below.

There it is we read and understand the wondrous words- "Whom the Lord loves He chastens." "Whom I love I rebuke and chasten." It is impossible to interpret the dark and mysterious dispensations of God's providence accurately but in the light of His love; and when thus seen and interpreted, we can, as with the hind's feet, walk firmly and safely upon the craggy and perilous places of adversity and trial, affliction and sorrow, each step luminous with His presence and vocal with His praise. "Every cloud that veils love, itself is love."

Oh, be not satisfied with walking in low shaded places- with but a faint and cold experience of God's love in your hearts; but climb in faith these high places, breathe their atmosphere, and bask in their warmth, comprehending with all saints what is the breadth, and length, and depth, and height of God's love in Christ Jesus, which passes knowledge, that you might be filled with all the fulness of God.

There are high places in Christ Jesus where God's saints, as with the hind's springing and cheerful foot, are made to walk. "I am the way," was the significant and gracious declaration of Jesus. In this "Way" the "new and living Way," which leads into the holiest, all God's saints walk; and thus walking as with the hind's confiding and gladsome step, they are "raised up together, and made to sit together in heavenly places in Christ Jesus." Yes, "heavenly places!" Such, is a sense of full pardon through His sin-atoning blood; such, is a sense of complete acceptance through His soul justifying righteousness; such, is the supply of His all-sufficient grace drawn from Himself, the infinite and inexhaustible Reservoir; such, too, the streams of sympathy and gentleness flowing from His human and compassionate nature, along all our pathway of suffering and sorrow.

Oh, these are indeed 'high places' in the Christian's travel through the wilderness and across the desert home to his Father in heaven! There is room for you, my reader, here. Do not walk at a distance from these 'high places,' viewing them from afar; but draw near, ascend, plant your feet on the 'stairs' (Song 2:14), the 'secret' of which you will thus learn, and with the hind's strong and firm foot ascend step by step until you reach the summit, and, pour forth your anthem of love and praise- "My soul does magnify the Lord, and my spirit has rejoiced in God my Savior."

And what true saint of God has not pressed, as with the hind's foot, the 'high places' of communion with God? "There is a path which no fowl knows, and which the vulture's eye has not seen." And there are paths, doubtless, untrodden even by the hind's venturous foot. But, here is a 'high place' where all the children of God travel, some with bolder and firmer foot than others; yet all leave their traces here. All are men and women of prayer; all have "entered into the holiest by the blood of Jesus, by the new and living way, which He has consecrated for us, through the veil, that is to say, His flesh;" all walk with God on these 'high places' of communion.

PRAYER raises the believer into the highest and holiest atmosphere. It would be impossible to reach a moral altitude of the soul loftier, purer, and brighter than this. The 'stairs' which, from the lowest depth, lead up to this hallowed height, are trodden and worn by the feet of many a Christian pilgrim, climbing with his burden and need, with his supplication and thanksgiving, to the mercy-seat. Well rewarded is he for his holy toil! Who has climbed these sacred 'stairs,' laden with sin, weary with care, pressed with neediness, crushed with sorrow, but has walked on these 'high places' with the hind's foot of strength and boldness, exclaiming with the Apostle, "Truly our fellowship is with the Father, and with His Son Jesus Christ."

Arise from your 'depths,' and give yourself to prayer! Uplift your eyes, dim with tears though they be, and gaze upon those sunny heights of divine communion towering above and smiling down upon you, and inviting your ascent. There sits your Father! there ministers your Intercessor! there rises the cloud of incense, prepared to perfume and secure the acceptance of your every petition- all encouraging you to plant your trembling foot upon the sacred 'stairs,' and "draw near with a true heart, and in full assurance of faith."

With such powerful attractions, and with such divine encouragements, alas! how we "restrain prayer before God!" How unbelievably, I had almost said, atheistically, we limit the power and goodness and veracity of God as the Answerer of Prayer! Alike ungrateful for the benefits we have received, and indifferent towards those we are still in expectation of, we neglect prayer, the only medium through which we can prove our gratitude to God.

"Who is it that has spread out the earth beneath our feet, opened paths to human industry across the waters, and hung the brilliant vault of the heavens above our heads? Who is it that directs my paths with the torch which enlightens me during the day? Who is it that makes the fountains spring up in the depths of the valleys? Who has dug out for our rivers the beds in which they are enclosed; has made the animal creation subservient to our necessities; has organized this vile dust; has given it at once life and intelligence; has engraved upon this handful of earth, of which I am composed, the resemblance of Divinity? and also, after this glorious image has been obscured and defaced by sin, who is it that has re-established it in its pristine beauty? MY FATHER!" (Gregory)

And yet we limit His power, distrust His faithfulness, and question His love, in hearing and answering PRAYER! Ascend, then, this sacred mount; walk with God upon these high places; cheered and strengthened by the words of Jesus: "Verily, verily, I say unto you, Whatever you shall ask the Father in my name, He will give it you..... Ask, and you shall receive, that your joy may be full."

And are there no high places of holy joy, of sweet repose and heavenly communion, where the saints may walk even in the midst of affliction and sorrow? Most assuredly there are. There are "high places" even in the valley, where God causes some of His sweetest springs to flow. Trials are steps heaven-ward; sorrows steps God-ward, in the experience of the saints. "When men are cast down, then you shall say, There is lifting up." The 'secret of the stairs' -God's hiding-place of His saints has often revealed the secret of His providence; and the mystery of His providence, thus made known, has in its turn unfolded the deeper mystery of His love.

Oh, it is often so, that the believer has never known how deeply God loves him, how truly a child of God he was, and how tender and faithful his Father's love, until God has afflicted him. Then he sees love, and nothing but love, in the calamity that has impoverished, in the disease that has wasted, in the bereavement that has crushed, in the fickleness that has changed. Love is the best interpreter of love, as its truest inspiration. The moment tried and sifted faith disentangles itself of second causes, and rests in God, that moment the bitter and unlovely bulb bursts into the sweet and beauteous flower, laden with the dew and bathed in the sunshine of heaven. It is thus that, sanctified sorrows yield to the believer the richest fruit; and that in the valley he drinks from sweeter springs than flow from the mountain's top!

Doubtless, the hind of the mountain often springs from rock to rock, from crag to crag, footsore and weary; the very feeling of pain and weakness rendering its bounds more cautious and its hold more sure. Thus does the believer walk in deep and sore trial. Wounded in heart, weary in spirit, and weakened in trial, he walks upon his high places of difficulty and danger warily, humbly, prayerfully. He is in the valley, and yet upon the mount: chastened and humbled under God's hand, he yet is in closer communion with his Father, more conscious of the sweet presence of his Savior, than when he trod the high places of worldly prosperity, and basked in the sunshine of creature good.

But, it is not always, and we write this for the comfort of God's tempted ones- that the saints of God accept this discipline of trial without murmur and rebellion. They too often lose sight of the wisdom that appoints, and the faithfulness that sends the trial, and the immense good to themselves it was designed to accomplish. Thus they refuse to walk in high places of fellowship with their Heavenly Father, beneath whose loving corrections they lie. As an old divine remarks, "The physician attacks the disease, and not the patient; his object is to cure him whom he causes to suffer. It is thus that God, whose mercy is infinite, chastises us only to bring us into the way of salvation, or to confirm our course in it. You are not angry with your physician when he applies the cautery or the knife to your gangrened limb; on the contrary, you can scarcely find language adequate to the expression of your gratitude; you keep repeating that he has saved your life by preventing the disease from spreading, and you pay him liberally for his attentions. Yet you murmur against the Lord, who wounds only for our good; and you are unwilling to acknowledge that the afflictions with which He visits us are the only means capable of restoring health to our souls, or of securing the continuance of it when it is restored to us."

Expect, then, the happiest results from this curative process of your Divine Physician. The prescription may be unpalatable, and the excision painful; nevertheless, the richest blessing to you and the highest glory to God will be the happy and hallowed result! "Every branch in me that bears not fruit He takes away, and every branch that bears fruit, He prunes, that it may bring forth more fruit." In this light, view you your present sickness, suffering, and sorrow. The medicine is prescribed by Jesus, the knife is in a Father's hand, and your song shall be-"He has done all things well."

"Heart, poor heart! while thus you are bleeding,
Faint and anguished is your needing,
Mercy for your life is pleading,
Dews of Pity round you shine;
And as Mercy, grace conferring,
Leads forth to Light the erring,
Hope your laden depths is stirring
With the might of Faith Divine
Griefs are gifts from Mercy's shrine,
You shall chaunt Amens for Thine."

Remember that the hinds' feet are to ascend. Learn this truth, that God has given you powerful elements of soul-ascension. You have feet shod with the preparation of the gospel of peace. You have wings of faith that can out-distance the eagle in its flight. Be not content, then, with a low standard of personal religion; with walking, where you may climb; with skimming the surface, when you may soar to the sun.

Ascend from your depths of darkness and doubt, of coldness and unbelief, and walk in your 'high places' of filial fellowship with God, of active service for Christ, of earnest self-denying labor for the conversion of sinners, of close communion with Eternal realities. "Arise, my love, my fair one, and come away. O my dove, that are in the clefts of the rock, in the secret Places of the stairs, let me see your countenance, let me hear your voice; for sweet is your voice, and your countenance is lovely."

Blessed are they who hide them in "the clefts of the Rock" -the wounds of Jesus; yet more blessed they who, in "the secret places of the stairs," are learning to ascend into a higher, purer, and sunnier region of spiritual life, entire consecration, and unclouded hope. Until death uncage your spirit, and your unclasped, uplifted wings bear you home to God, be much in the 'clefts of the rock,' in the 'secret of the stairs,' and with hinds' feet walking on the high places of God. Then shall the promise be fulfilled in your experience- "He shall dwell on high (margin, heights, or high places): his place of defense shall be the munitions of rocks: bread shall be given him; his waters shall be sure."

Lord, I would sincerely bend my ear to Your sweet, all-persuasive voice- "ARISE, MY LOVE, MY FAIR ONE, AND COME AWAY."

"Oh, I am heavy laden! Faith's eye is growing dim;
I wander on in darkness, groping in vain for Him;
For Him whom my soul loveth, for Him who died to be
A sacrifice for sinners, a Fount of life to me.

"Sweet dove of downy plumage, I pray you bid me hide
In clefted rocky shadows, close to Your wounded side!
Your voice of silver sweetness, Your face of beauty rare,
I seek in secret places the- 'secret of the stair.'

"I hear them! hear the sweet words, He whispereth to me
His words of loving welcome, forgiveness full and free.
Once more His face appeareth, in answer to my prayers,
And thus in joy I learn it, that 'secret of the stairs.'

"That precious, precious secret- He writes it deep within
Of peace and joy abounding, and victory over sin;
But in the inner temple, where burns the altar flame,
In word of light is graven, His new, His wondrous name.

"The 'stairs' were painful climbing, when first my weary feet
Essayed, untried, to mount them, an unknown God to meet;
But now His arm is round me, and light and free as air,
I mount with wing unwearied, and reach the topmost 'stair.'

"O Lord of life unending, of daily life the key,
Be food, and drink, and manna, and living grace to me!
Walk with me all my journey, be round me everywhere;
But give Your conscious presence, in 'secret on the stair.'

"For life is ever cloud-land, and only they who know
Your guiding eye can follow, where You would have them go.

One secret of the staircase, appears a beacon star
To shine upon Your pilgrims, to guide them from afar.
    "And fierce and sharp the battle, which those who would engage
To be Your crested warriors, for life and death must wage;
But armor of God's forging, which every conqueror wears,
Is stored in secret places, the 'secret of the stairs.'
    "When sorrow's chilling fingers, turn hearts and memories cold,
When sad remembrance lingers, on voices loved of old,
Lo, on the 'stairs' there sits, all white in angel sheen,
Pale Resignation singing sweet, hymns our sobs between.
    "A storehouse overflowing, with choicest heavenly things,
From which the dear Lord daily, His priceless mercy brings;
A sheltered nook where comes; nor doubt, nor fear, nor care,
Earth knows no safer hiding, than that behind the 'stair.'
    "Dead world, there is a secret, known only unto me,
A sweet and thrilling secret- I cannot tell it thee;
But if you too would learn it, would catch it unawares,
Go, seek as I have sought it, 'in places of the stairs.'
    "O Dove! my Dove I know You! I see Your lovely face,
I hear Your honeyed accents; of truth, and love, and grace;
The smile of peace You give; is fair, exceeding fair;
This is the choicest 'secret' that lingers on the 'stair.'
    "No more I walk in darkness, no more my footsteps stray;
The Rock whose cooling shadow, falls over all my way,
Is full of clefts for hiding, and secrets of the stair,
And rest is mine, and glory; the Lord is with me there!
    "Here hiding safe forever, within this sacred shade,
Nor sin, nor death, nor torment; can bid me be afraid;
 For I have learned the 'secret'; sought long with tears and prayers,
A present help Christ dwells in, the 'places of the stairs.'
(Mary Winslow)

Printed in Great Britain
by Amazon